Basket Quilt Show

7

Prize-Winning Wall Hangings

Bobbie Matela, Managing Editor; Carol Wilson Mansfield, Art Director;
Linda Causee, Editor; Meredith Montross, Associate Editor;
Terea Mitchell, Illustrations
Graphic Solutions, Book Design

ISBN: 0-88195-643-0
Printed in U. S. A.
1 2 3 4 5 6 7 8 9

Introduction

"The sequel is never as good as the original book," I told myself as I drove up to the corporate offices of House of Fabrics. I had been invited once again to help judge their annual quilt competition. Last year the winning log cabin quilts had so stimulated my creative juices that I insisted that we had to share those quilts with the world, and thus the ***Log Cabin Quilt Show*** (ASN Book #4149) was born. "This year's contest, based on the theme of baskets, could not possibly rival last year's competition," I convinced myself.

Was I mistaken!

The offices at corporate headquarters were once again filled with a breathtaking display of quilt art that left me reeling. How could these quilters conceive of and then produce such unbelievable variations on the simple theme of a basket, all the while making certain that their corners met and their quilting stitches were perfectly even?

We didn't really plan a second book, but standing there in that room with those wonderful quilts, I knew immediately that ***Basket Quilt Show*** had to be published.

Since none of these quilters intended her quilt to be included in an instructional book, we could only include those quilts which lent themselves to complete instructions. In a few cases we had to take the liberty of simplifying the design so that our readers would be able to approximate the original.

Luckily we were able to include all of the first four prize winners from Linda Anderson's grand prize "Rosy Baskets," which was so perfectly executed to Millie K. Frese's delightful and amusing first prize "Magic Sewing Basket." We all loved the exquisite second prize winner, "Jeannie's Summer Basket" by Shirley Kraus, and the simply charming third prize "Mae's Baskets" by Nancy Wagner Graves.

We have also included Sheri Wilkinson Lalk's honorable mention quilt, her traditional "Baltimore Basket." In addition, I could not omit two finalists that did not place in the prize winners but were special favorites of mine, "Des Paniers Bleus" by Julia Cousins and "Heirloom Basket" by Ruth Diane Hosfield. Julia was so creative in her use of blue fabrics that I knew many quilters would want to recreate her quilt. Ruth's adaptation of an Anne Orr pattern had to be included because I am a long-time admirer of the work of Anne Orr, a famous needlework designer of the early half of the twentieth century.

Rita Weiss

Contents

General Directions

Choosing the Fabric

Old time quilts were traditionally made of 100% cotton, and this is still the fabric that experienced quilters prefer.

Cotton has a number of properties that makes it especially suitable for patchwork. You will find less distortion with cotton fabric which means that your carefully cut small pieces will fit together more easily. If you make a mistake and find a puckered area, a quilt made from 100% cotton often can be ironed flat with a steam iron. In addition, the needle moves through cotton with ease as opposed to some synthetics. If you are hand quilting, this is an extremely valuable quality.

Pre-washing fabric is not necessary, but it is necessary to test your fabric to make certain that the fabric is colorfast and preshrunk (don't trust those manufacturer's labels). Start by cutting a 2"-wide strip (cut crosswise) of each of the fabrics that you have selected for your quilt. To determine whether the fabric is colorfast, put each strip separately into a clean bowl of extremely hot water, or hold the fabric strip under hot running water. If your fabric bleeds a great deal, all is not necessarily lost. It might only be necessary to wash all of the fabric until all of the excess dye has washed out. Fabrics which continue to bleed after they have been washed several times should be eliminated.

To test for shrinkage, take each saturated strip and iron it dry with a hot iron. When the strip is completely dry, measure and compare it to your original measurements. The fabric industry allows about 2% shrinkage in cotton fabrics. That means that your 45" crosswise fabric should not lose more than 1". If all of your fabric strips shrink about the same amount, then you really have no problem. When you wash your finished quilt, you may achieve the puckered look of an antique quilt. If you do not want this look, you will have to wash and dry all of the fabric before beginning so that shrinkage is no longer a problem. If only one of your fabrics is shrinking more than the others, it will have to be washed and dried, or discarded.

Fabrics should also be tested for sun fading. Put samples of fabric in the window of the room where your quilt will be used, or—if uncertain—in your sunniest window. After a few days of very strong sunlight, compare fabrics. If there are changes in color, either discard the fabric, or decide that you're going to like the color as it changes.

Make sure that your fabric is absolutely square. If it is not, you will have difficulty cutting your strips. Fabric is woven with crosswise and lengthwise threads. Lengthwise threads should be parallel to the selvage (that's the finished edge along the sides; sometimes the fabric company prints its name along the selvage) and crosswise threads should be perpendicular to the selvage. If fabric is off-grain, you can straighten it. Pull gently on the true bias in the opposite direction to the off-grain edge. Continue doing this until crosswise threads are at a right angle to lengthwise threads.

Using Templates

Some of the quilts in this collection require patterns for piecing; in quilting, patterns are called "templates."

***Note:** The template patterns for piecing are printed with seam allowance. The patterns for appliqué are printed without seam allowance.*

To make templates for piecing, lay a piece of tracing paper over the pattern pieces in the book and carefully trace the pattern pieces. For hand piecing, trace pattern along dashed line and add 1/4" seam allowance all around when cutting from fabric. For machine piecing, trace pattern along solid line and use a consistent 1/4" seam allowance when sewing. (Do not photocopy the pieces instead of tracing. Photocopy machines are not exact, and your pieces may not fit together.) Carefully glue your tracing onto heavy cardboard or plastic. Special plastic for making templates is available in quilt, craft or stationery stores. If you use a clear plastic, you can trace directly onto plastic and eliminate the gluing.

Once you have made your template, carefully cut it out. It is important that your templates be cut out carefully because if they are not accurate, the patchwork will not fit together. Use a pair of good-size sharp scissors (not the same scissors that you use to cut fabric), a single-edged razor blade or a craft knife. Be careful not to bend the corners of the triangles.

Hold your pencil or marker at an angle so that the point is against the side of the template and trace around the template. Continue moving the template and tracing it on fabric the required number of times, moving from left to right and always keeping straight lines parallel with grain.

You can use your rotary cutter to cut several layers at once. Fold fabric so you have as many layers as the number of pieces needed. Lay your template on the wrong side of the fabric which has been folded. Place it so that as many straight sides of the piece as possible are parallel to the crosswise and lengthwise grain of the fabric. Now trace around the template. Then use your acrylic ruler and rotary cutter along the traced lines, making certain that you cut away from your body.

Machine Piecing

Machine piecing is done with the straight stitch foot and throat place on the machine. Set your machine for about ten stitches to the inch and use a size 14 needle. The quilts in this book use 1/4" seam allowance (unless stated otherwise), so you are going to need some way to make sure that you sew with a perfect 1/4" seam. If your machine has the 1/4" marked on the throat plate, you are in luck. If not, measure 1/4" from the needle hole to the right side of the presser foot and place a piece of tape on the plate. Keep the edge of your piece lined up with the tape and you will be able to sew a perfect 1/4" seam.

To speed up the sewing process, use chain piecing. When you have sewn the first pieces together, don't end your thread; just continue feeding the next piece. When you have finished chain piecing your first two pieces, snip them apart. Don't worry about threads coming undone; they will eventually be anchored by cross seams.

Blocking the Blocks

When you have completed a block, it must be "blocked" before it is joined to another block. The term "blocking" means keeping the edges straight on all sides of the quilt so it will be a perfect square or rectangle when finished. The term applies to the quilt's parts as well as to an entire quilt, so the blocking process is a continuous one from start to finish.

Place the completed block on the ironing board and pull the edges straight with your fingers. Cover the block with a damp cloth and steam with a warm iron (or use a steam iron). Iron the block perfectly flat with no puckers starting with the edges first and the center last. Move the iron as little as possible to keep the block from stretching.

Joining the Blocks

After you have pieced and blocked the required number of blocks for your quilt, lay them out to get the final effect before sewing them together.

Using the 1/4" seam allowance, join the blocks in horizontal or vertical rows. When rows are completed, join two rows together, matching seam lines. Then add additional rows.

Hint: *When crossing seams, be especially careful to match seam to seam. One learns to do this fairly accurately while sewing by feeling with the fingers. It helps if the lower seam is turned one way and the top seam the other, so press seams for odd numbered rows in one direction; even numbered in the other.*

Basic Appliqué

Traditional Basting Method

1. Trace pattern piece on right side of fabric and mark around the piece, using the proper marking tool. Measure 1/4" around the shape and draw a second line. This second line is your cutting line. As you become more proficient, you will be able to add this 1/4" seam allowance purely by eye.

2. Cut shape out of fabric with a good sharp scissors.

3. Turn under seam allowance and finger press the turned-under edges in place. Baste the edges as you turn them, keeping your finger pressing about an inch ahead of the needle. The thread that you use for basting should be enough of a contrast so that you can see the thread for removal when the appliqué is finally attached. However, be careful of using a dark-colored thread on light fabric as this may leave some marking when the basting is removed. Edges which fit underneath other pieces do not need to have seam allowances turned under.

5. Concave curves should be clipped so that the seam allowance will flatten when turned under. A concave curve is an edge that goes inward. Make as few clips as possible because the cutting can cause the fabric to fray. Clip curves only as you come to them to prevent fraying.

Hint: *Make a few cuts, then turn under the seam allowance and check to see how flat the piece is lying. If the edge is not flat enough, make a few more cuts.*

6. Convex curves are never clipped. A convex curve is an edge that goes outward from the shape.

7. Pin each patch into place and, if desired, baste onto the quilt block. Pieces which fit under other pieces should be placed down first. When entire block is pinned or basted in place, sew pieces to block along fold using blindstitch, **Fig 1**. Go up at A, catching one or two threads of folded applique piece; go

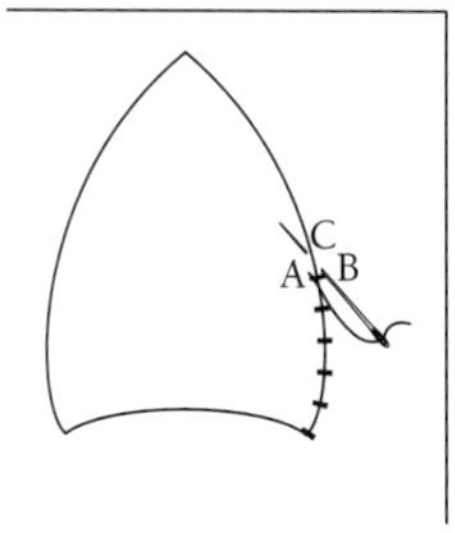

C
A
B

Fig 1

back down at B into background fabric (quilt top), next to fold. Come back up through background about 1/8" away at C, catching one to two threads into folded applique. Continue around entire piece.

Freezer Paper Appliqué

1. Trace pattern pieces as directed in individual project onto freezer paper; cut out.

2. Place pattern pieces shiny side up on wrong side of desired fabric; cut out pattern pieces adding 1/8" to 1/4" seam allowance all around.

3. Fold seam allowance over freezer paper toward shiny side; press edge with hot, dry iron, **Fig 2**. If there is a pointed tip on an appliqué piece, fold edge at tip first, **Fig 3**, then continue folding and pressing.

Fig 2

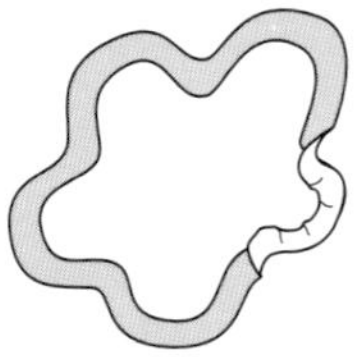

Fig 3

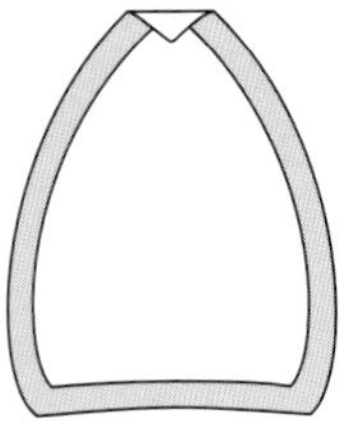

4. Remove freezer paper.

5. Place appliqué piece in position on quilt top; baste or pin in place. Stitch appliqué piece in place using blindstitch.

Adding Borders

Although we give measurements for border strips, we recommend that before cutting your border strips, measure the finished quilt top and cut your borders to the exact size. If you have made some mistakes in the piecing (for instance, if you made your blocks with a larger than 1/4" seam allowance) this will be the time to adjust your border measurements.

Using the 1/4" seam allowance, attach one side border to the right side of the quilt and one to the left. Then attach the top and bottom borders. Use the 1/4" seam allowance at all times. Repeat for additional borders.

Preparing the Quilt Top

Give the quilt top a final blocking, making sure all corners are square and all seams are pressed to one side.

We have made suggestions for quilting your quilt, but you may wish to follow your own quilting plan. However if you are planning to quilt your top, you will need to mark the quilting pattern before joining the top to the batting.

If you prefer to tie your quilt, skip the next section on marking the quilting design.

Marking the Quilting Design

Before marking on your quilt top, **be sure to test any marking material to make sure it will wash out of your fabric.** Mark all quilting lines on the right side of the fabric. For marking use a hard lead pencil, chalk or other special quilt marking materials. If you quilt right on the marked lines, they will not show.

A word of caution: *Marking lines which are intended to disappear after quilting - either by exposure to air or with water - may become permanent when set with a hot iron. Therefore, don't iron your quilt top after you have marked your quilting pattern.*

If you are quilting around shapes, you may not need to mark your line if you feel that you can accurately gauge the quilting line as you work. If you are quilting "in the ditch" of the seam (the space right in the seam), marking is not necessary. Other quilting patterns will need to be marked.

Attaching Batting and Backing

There are a number of different types of batting on the market. Very thin batting will require a great deal of quilting to hold it (quilting lines no more than 1" apart); very thick batting should be used only for tied quilts.

If you are planning to machine quilt, you should investigate the new battings on the market which are intended for machine quilting.

We have indicated the amount of fabric required for the backing in each pattern. If you prefer another fabric, buy a backing fabric that is soft and loosely woven so that the quilting needle can pass through easily. Bed sheets are usually not good backing materials.

Since some of the quilts in this book are wider than fabric width, you will have to sew lengths together to make your quilt backing. Cut off selvages and seam pieces together carefully; iron seam open. This is the only time in making a quilt that seams should be pressed open.

Cut batting and backing larger than the quilt top; about 2" wider than quilt top on all sides. Place backing, wrong side up, on flat surface. Place batting on top of this, matching outer edges.

Hint: *Remove batting from its packaging a day in advance and open it out full size. This will help the batting to lie flat.*

The layers of the quilt must be held together before quilting. There are two methods for doing this: thread basting and safety pin basting.

For **thread basting:** First, place backing wrong side up, then batting; center quilt top, right side up, on top of the batting. Baste with long stitches, starting in the center and sewing toward the edges in a number of diagonal lines.

For **safety pin basting:** Layer the backing, batting and quilt top and pin through all three layers at once. Because you don't have to put your hand under the quilt as you do when you are thread basting, the quilt top does not move out of position. Start pinning from center and work out to edges, placing pins no more than 4" to 6" apart. Think of your quilt plan as you work and make certain that your pins avoid prospective quilting lines. Choose rustproof pins that are size #1 or #2. To make pinning easier, many quilters use a quilter's spoon. The spoon is notched, so that it can push the point of the safety pin closed.

Quilting

The quilts in this collection can be hand or machine quilted. If you have never used a sewing machine for quilting, you might want to read some more about the technique. *Quilting for People Who Don't Have Time to Quilt* (Book #4111) by Marti Michell and *A Beginner's Guide to Machine Quilting* (Book #4121) by Judi Tyrrell, both published by ASN Publishing, are excellent introductions to machine quilting. These books are available at your local quilt store or department, or write the publisher for a list of sources.

You do not need a special machine for quilting. You can machine quilt with almost any home sewing machine. Just make sure that it is in good working order and that the presser foot is not set for too much pressure which can cause rippling. An even-feed foot is a good investment if you are going to machine quilt since it feeds the top and bottom layers through the machine evenly.

Use fine transparent nylon thread in the top and regular sewing thread in the bobbin.

To **quilt-in-the-ditch** of a seam (this is actually stitching in the space between two pieces of fabric that have been sewn together), use your hands to pull the blocks or pieces apart and machine stitch right between the two pieces. Try to keep your stitching just to the side of the seam that does not have the bulk of the seam allowance under it. When you have finished stitching, the quilting will be practically hidden in the seam.

Free form machine quilting is done with a darning foot and the feed dogs down on your sewing machine. It can be used to quilt around a design or to quilt a motif. Mark your quilting design as described in Marking the Quilting Design on page 5. Free form machine quilting takes practice to master because you are controlling the quilt through the machine rather than the machine moving the quilt. With free form machine quilting you can quilt in any direction—up and down, side to side and even in circles without pivoting the quilt around the needle.

Attaching the Binding

Place the quilt on a flat surface and carefully trim the backing and batting 1/2" beyond the quilt top edge. Measure the quilt top and cut two 2"-wide binding strips the length of your quilt (for sides). Right sides together, sew one side strip to one side of the quilt with 1/4" seam allowance (seam allowance should be measured from outer edge of quilt top fabric, not outer edge of batting/backing). Turn binding to back and turn under 1/4" on raw edge; slipstitch to backing. Do other side in same manner. For top and bottom edge binding strips, measure carefully adding 1/2" to each end; cut strips 2" wide. To eliminate raw edges at corners, turn the extra 1/2" to wrong side before stitching to top and bottom. Finish in same manner as sides.

Rosy Baskets

by Linda J. Anderson
Grand Prize
Approximate Size: 43" x 43"

"The basket block pattern was taken from an old book. The remainder of the quilt was my own design."

Fabric Requirements:

1 1/2 yds 90"-wide muslin (background and backing)
1 1/2 yds black print fabric (baskets, squares and binding)
1 yd lt rose print (squares)
1 yd dk rose print (squares, flowers, tulips)
1/8 yd very dk rose print (flower and tulip centers)
1/8 yd green print (leaves)
batting

Pattern Pieces (page 12):

A Basket
B Flower
C Flower Center
D Tulip
E Tulip Center
F Large Leaf
G Small Leaf
H Square
I Large Triangle
J Small Triangle

Cutting Requirements:

four 12 1/2" squares, muslin
four 2 1/2"-wide crosswise strips*, black print
four 1 3/8" x 20" bias strips for basket handles, black print
sixteen Large Triangles (I), black print
four Small Triangles (J), black print
four Baskets (A), black print
eight 2 1/2"-wide crosswise strips*, lt rose print
40 Large Triangles (I), lt rose print
six 2 1/2"-wide crosswise strips*, dk rose print
four Flowers (B), dk rose print
eight Tulips (D), dk rose print
four Flower Centers (C), very dk rose print
eight Tulip Centers (E), very dk rose print
eight Large Leaves (F), green print
eight Small Leaves (G), green print

**If you would like to cut individual squares using pattern pieces, cut the following and refer to Layout and Figs for placement:*
*57 H Squares, black print**
*112 H Squares, dk rose print**
*108 H Squares, lt rose print**

Instructions

Basket Block

1. Draw appliqué design on right side of 12 1/2" background square using pattern pieces and referring to placement diagram, **Fig 1**.

D
E
F
G
C
B
A
Fig 1

2. Prepare basket, basket handle, flower, tulips and leaves for appliqué (see Basic Appliqué, pages 5 and 6).

3. Appliqué in numerical sequence, **Fig 2**.

1
2
3
2
5
4
7
8
6
4
2
3
2
5
Fig 2

4. Repeat steps 1 to 3 for three more Basket Blocks.

Shown in color on back cover

Piecing the Quilt

1. For patchwork sashing and frame around blocks, sew a black print strip to a lt rose print strip, **Fig 3**; press seam toward dk fabric. Repeat with two more pairs of strips.

2. Cut strips at 2 1/2" intervals for pairs of squares, **Fig 4**. You will need 36 pairs.

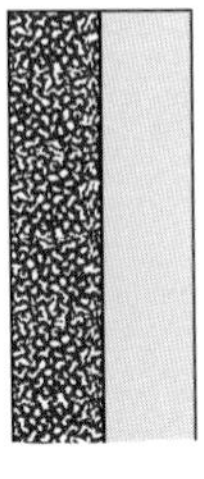

Fig 3

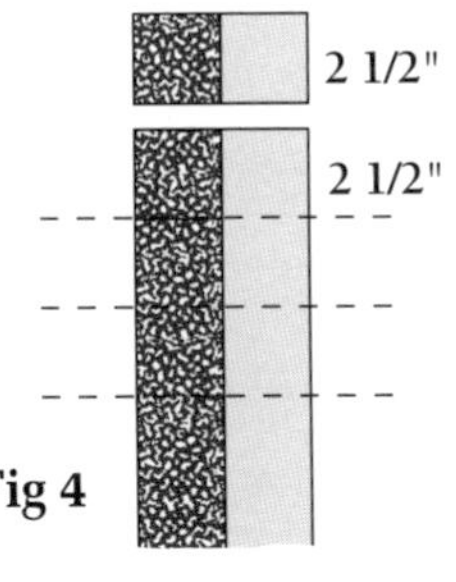
2 1/2"
2 1/2"

Fig 4

3. Sew three pairs together, **Fig 5**; repeat three more times.

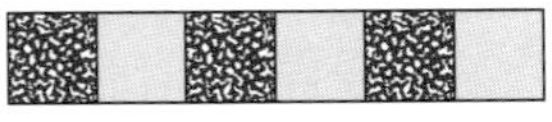

Fig 5

4. Sew a Basket Block to both long sides of pieced strip, **Fig 6**; repeat turning pieced strip upside down, **Fig 7**.

Fig 6

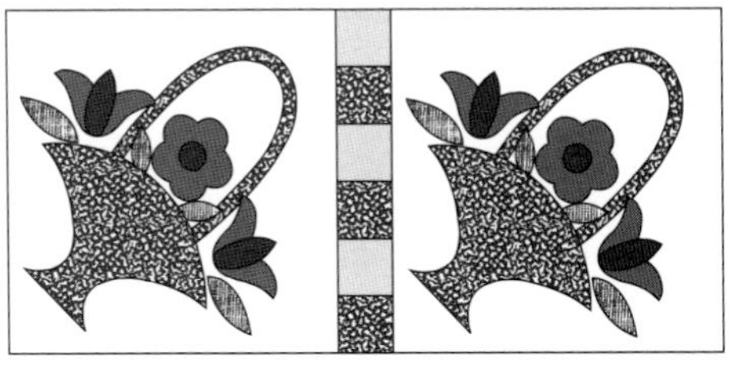

Fig 7

5. Sew pieced strip to opposite sides of a black print square, **Fig 8**; sew to Basket blocks, **Fig 9**.

Fig 8

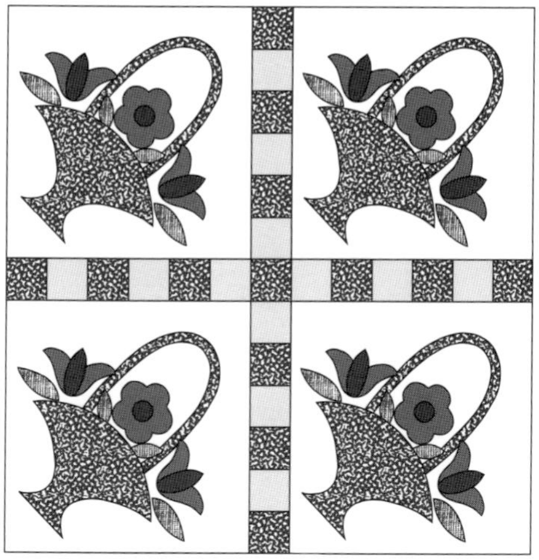

Fig 9

6. Sew six pairs of squares together; sew lt rose square to one end, **Fig 10**. Repeat for one more strip. Sew strips to opposite sides of quilt.

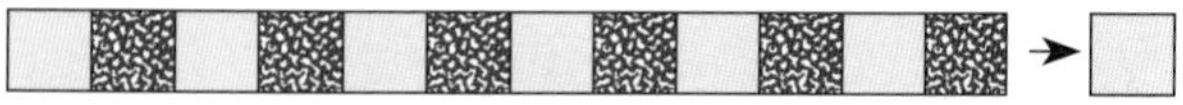

Fig 10

7. Sew seven pairs of squares together; sew black print square to one end, **Fig 11**. Sew strips to remaining two sides of quilt, **Fig 12**.

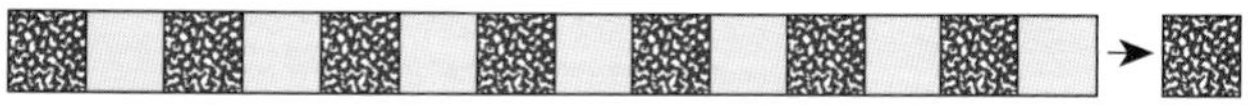

Fig 11

Fig 12

8. For large pieced corner triangles, sew a lt and a dk rose strip together, **Fig 13**. Repeat with four more pairs of strips.

9. Cut strips at 2 1/2" intervals for pairs of squares, **Fig 14**. You will need 68 pairs.

Fig 13

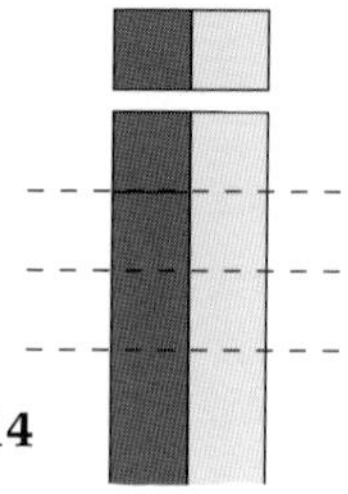

Fig 14

10. Sew a dk rose strip and a black print strip together; cut at 2 1/2" intervals, **Fig 15**. You will need 16 pairs.

11. Sew pairs of squares in rows: first row has six pairs, second row has five pairs, third row has four pairs, fourth row has three pairs, fifth row has two pairs and sixth row has one pair. Add a dk rose print square at one end of each row, **Fig 16**. Sew lt rose print triangles at each end of first five rows; sew black print triangles at each end of sixth row and to each side of a dark rose print square, **Fig 17**.

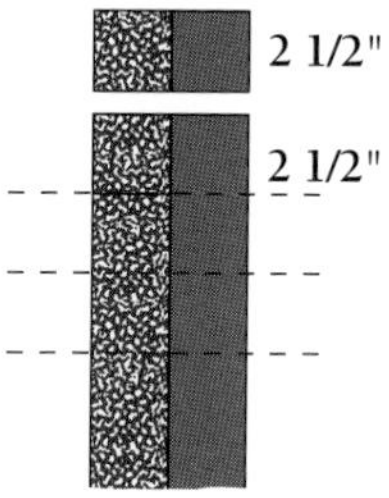
2 1/2"
2 1/2"

Fig 15

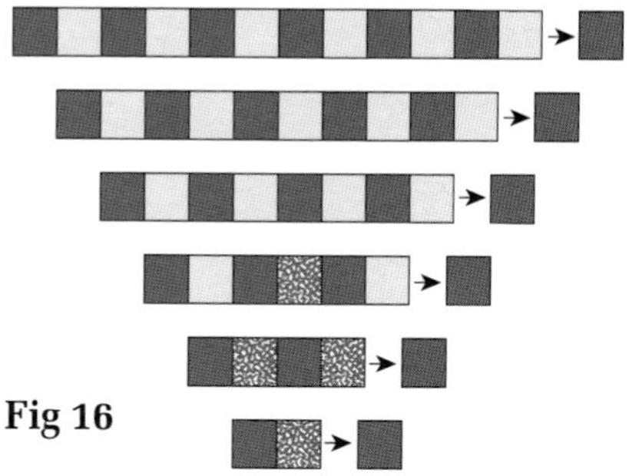

Fig 16

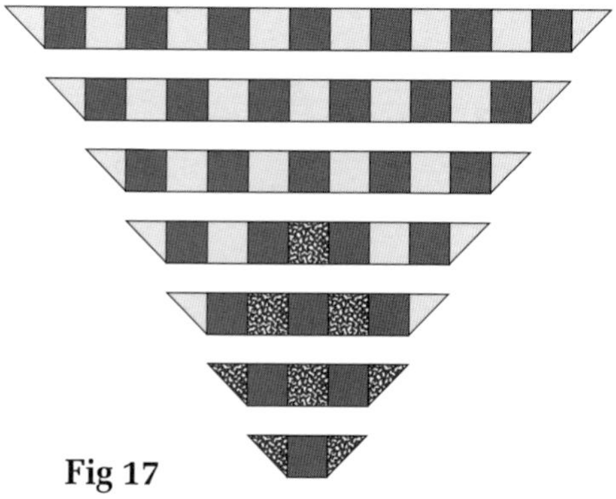

Fig 17

12. Sew rows together adding black print triangle (J) to finish corner, **Fig 18**.

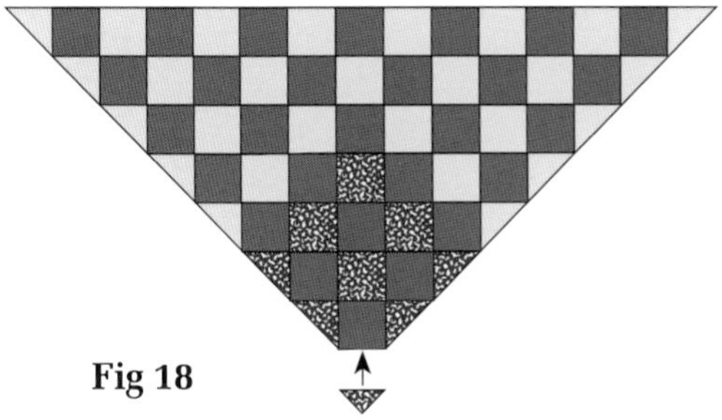

Fig 18

13. Repeat steps 11 and 12 for three more corners. Referring to Layout, sew corner triangles to central basket section complete quilt top.

Finishing the Quilt

See General Directions starting with Preparing the Quilt Top, pages 6 and 7, to complete your quilt. Photographed quilt was quilted 1/4" from inside edge of each square; basket blocks were quilted along edges of baskets and flowers with cross hatching (1" apart) outside the baskets.

Quilt Layout

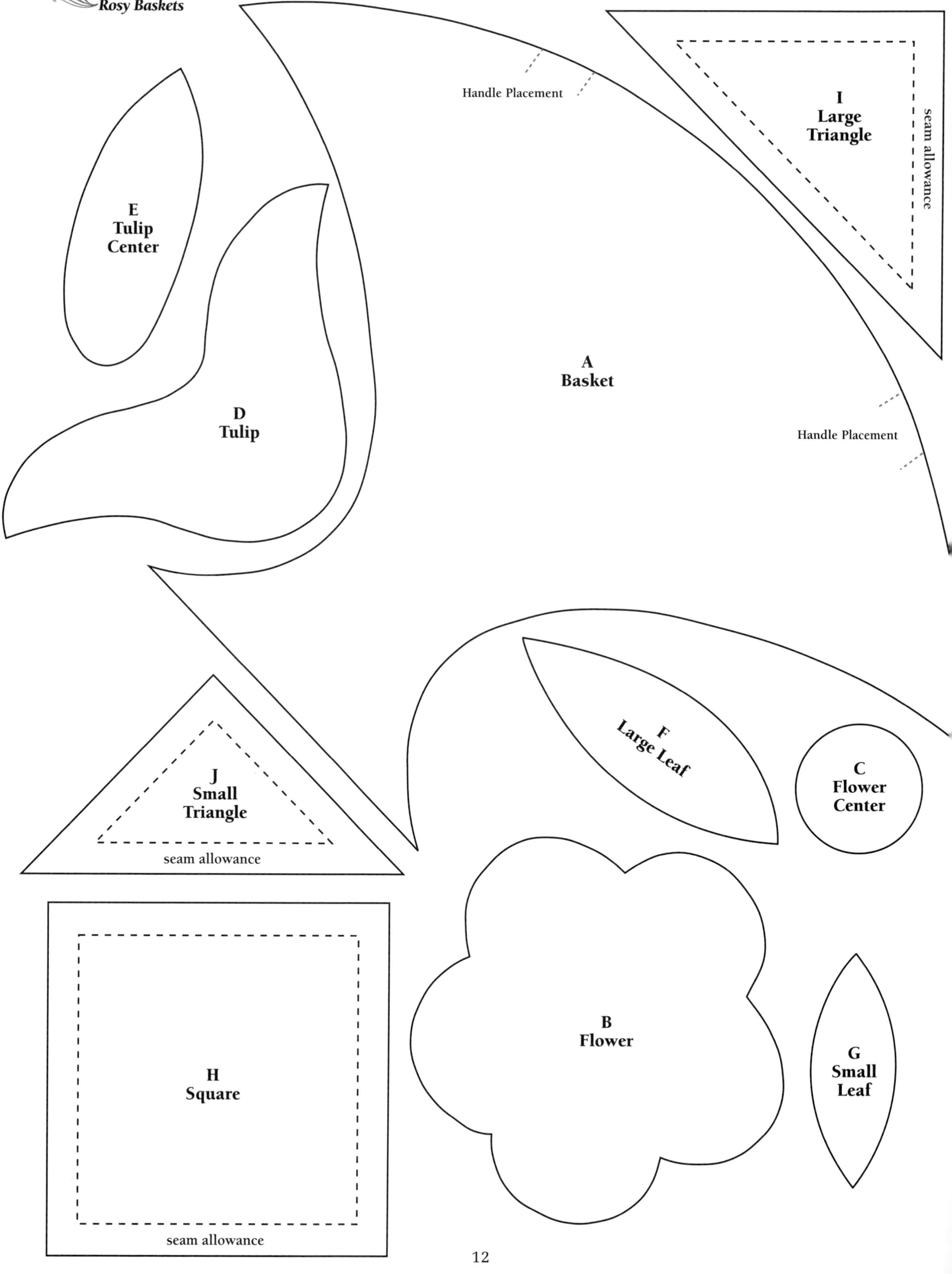
A
Basket
Handle Placement
Handle Placement
I
Large
Triangle
seam allowance
E
Tulip
Center
D
Tulip
F
Large Leaf
C
Flower
Center
J
Small
Triangle
seam allowance
B
Flower
G
Small
Leaf
H
Square
seam allowance

Shown in color on page 43

Magic Sewing Basket

by Millie K. Frese
First Prize
Approximate Size: 40 1/2" x 40 1/2"

"Basketweaving and quilting are two of my favorite hobbies, so this was a contest I couldn't resist. But Magic Sewing Basket *represents more than a contest entry for me—it's a snapshot of sorts that tells a story.*

"Several years ago I began handpiecing a Grandmother's Flower Garden *quilt. It was my very first quilting attempt. The pattern called for more than 2,600 hexagons. Undaunted, I began cutting and stitching. Since then, I've completed several bed quilts, quilted wall hangings and crib quilts, but the* Flower Garden *quilt top remains incomplete. Hundreds of hexagons rest in one of my handwoven baskets, waiting patiently for the attention I occasionally offer.If only I could weave a little magic into that basket and rouse the sleepy calico petals to life. Then they'd sew themselves together around bright yellow centers and dance their way out of the basket into an enchanted fabric bouquet.*

"This animated fantasy, along with a pad of graph paper and a few sharpened pencils, was all I needed to begin. I framed my Magic Sewing Basket *with scaled-down versions of some of my favorite traditional quilt block patterns, incorporating an array of calicos to give it a scrap quilt flavor. Perhaps some day the scraps from the* Magic Sewing Basket *will become petals in my slowly emerging garden."*

Fabric Requirements:

For scrap Sampler Blocks, Grandmother's Flower Garden blocks and Partial Grandmother's Flower Garden blocks, Spool, and Scissors Handles:

1/8 yd each of twelve or more fabrics (Use additional fabrics from your scrap bag to weave fragments of your own quilting history into your quilt. More than 30 fabrics were used in the sampler border.)

For Central Basket:

1/4 yd lt brown solid
1/4 yd brown print
1/8 yd med brown solid
1/4 yd dk brown solid
1/8 yd neutral print

Additional:

1/2 yd dk print for narrow inside border and binding
1 yd printed muslin for background
1 1/3 yd muslin for backing
gold lamé scrap for needle
silver lamé scrap for scissor blades
embroidery floss for thread and for lashing the basket rim
batting

Pattern Pieces (pages 18 to 20):

For Piecing

A Basket Diamond
B Nine Patch Square
C Spool Trapezoid
D Spool Square
E Pinwheel Triangle
F Small Star Square
G Small Star Triangle
H Large Star Triangle
I Large Star Square
J Basket Rectangle
K Large Basket Triangle
L Lower Basket Triangle
M Small Basket Triangle
N Flower Garden Hexagon

For Appliqué

O Upper/Lower Spool
P Spool Rectangle
Q Front Handle
R Back Handle
S Needle
T Right Scissors Handle
U Left Scissors Handle
V Top Scissors Blade
W Bottom Scissors Blade
X Appliqué Heart
Y Small Basket Handle

Cutting Requirements:

Background, Border, Binding

two 1 1/2" x 28 1/2" strips, dk print (border)
two 1 1/2" x 30 1/2" strips, dk print (border)
four 2" x 44" strips, dk print (binding)
one 28 1/2" x 28 1/2" square, muslin (background)

Central Basket

three 1 1/2" x 26" strips, lt brown solid (central basket)
one Front Handle (Q), lt brown solid (central basket)
three 1 1/2" x 26" strips, brown print (central basket)
twelve Basket Diamonds (A), brown print
twelve Basket Diamonds (A), med brown solid
1"-wide bias strips for basket rim, dk brown solid
one Back Handle (R), dk brown solid
one 3" x 18 1/2" strip, neutral print

Nine Patch Block

twenty Nine Patch Squares (B), dk print
sixteen Nine Patch Squares (B), lt print

Appliqué Heart Block

four 5 1/2" squares, print
four Appliqué Hearts (X), contrasting print

Spool Block

twelve Spool Trapezoids (C), spool fabric
twelve Spool Trapezoids (C), background fabric
six Spool Squares (D), spool fabric

Pinwheel Block

sixteen Pinwheel Triangles (E), dk print
sixteen Pinwheel Triangles (E), lt print

Star Block

sixteen Small Star Squares (F), background fabric
32 Small Star Triangles (G), star fabric
sixteen Large Star Triangles (I), background fabric
four Large Star Squares (I), star fabric

Basket Block

twelve Basket Rectangles (J), background fabric
six Lower Basket Triangles (L), background fabric
twelve Small Basket Triangles (M), basket fabric
six Large Basket Triangles (K), basket fabric
six Large Basket Triangles (K), background fabric
six Small Basket Handles (Y), basket fabric

Grandmother's Flower Garden

76 Hexagons (N), assorted fabrics

Additional Pieces

one Left Scissors Handle (U), turquoise print
one Right Scissors Handle (T), turquoise print
one Top Scissors Blade (V), silver lamé
one Bottom Scissors Blade (W), silver lamé
one Needle (S), gold lamé

Instructions

Center Basket Section

1. Sew a 1 1/2"-wide lt brown strip on opposite long sides of a brown print strip for Set 1, **Fig 1**; press seams toward darker fabric. Sew a brown print strip on opposite sides of a lt brown strip for Set 2, **Fig 2**; press seams toward darker fabric.

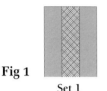

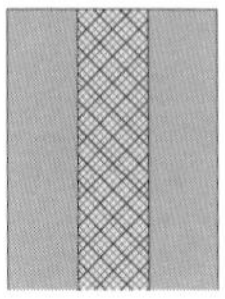
Fig 1
Set 1

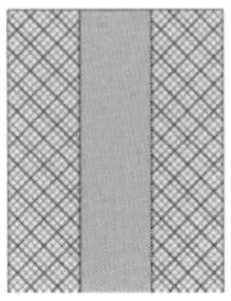
Fig 2
Set 2

2. Cut fourteen of each set at 1 1/2" intervals and one at 2", **Fig 3**.

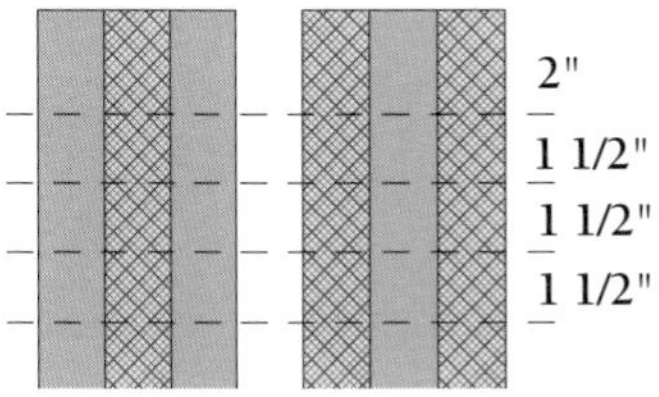
2"
1 1/2"
1 1/2"
1 1/2"
Fig 3

3. Sew two 1 1/2"-wide strips from Set 1 to one 1 1/2"-wide strip from Set 2 to form Nine Patch 1, **Fig 4**. Repeat for a total of four blocks.

4. Sew two 1 1/2"-wide strips from Set 2 to one 1 1/2" strip from Set 1 to form Nine Patch 2, **Fig 5**. Repeat for a total of four blocks.

5. Sew two 1 1/2" strips from Set 1 to the 2"-wide strip from Set 2 to form Nine Patch 3; sew two 1 1/2"-wide strips from Set 2 to the 2"-wide strip from Set 1, **Fig 6**.

Nine Patch 1
Fig 4

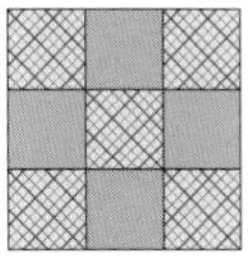
Nine Patch 2
Fig 5

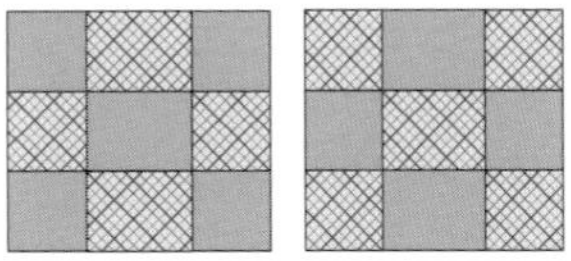
Nine Patch 3 Nine Patch 4
Fig 6

6. Sew Nine Patches to form basket, **Fig 7**.

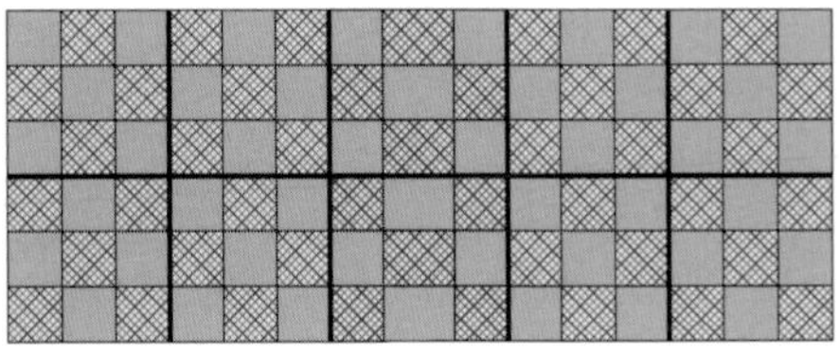
Fig 7

7. Sew Diamonds (C), alternating colors, in six rows of four; sew rows together, **Fig 8**.

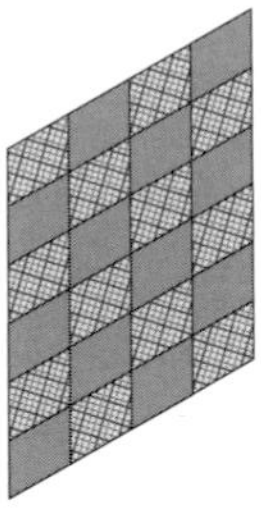
Fig 8

8. Sew C Diamond section to right side of basket, **Fig 9**. Press seam allowances under on side and bottom edges only; top edges will be covered with bias strips.

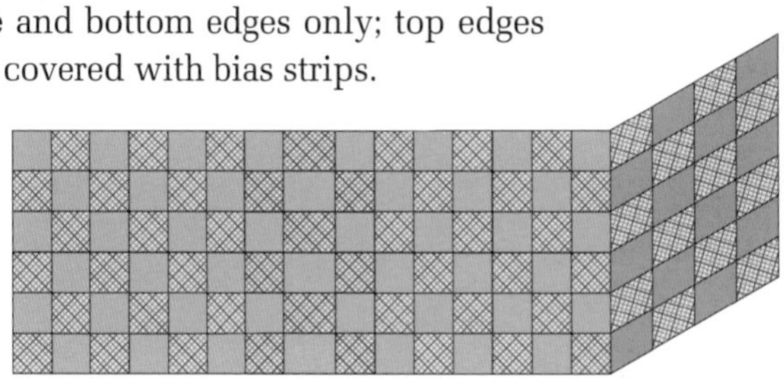
Fig 9

9. For Grandmother's Flower Garden Blocks, mark 1/4" seam allowance on wrong side of each hexagon. Hand piece one hexagon to each side of center hexagon for middle row stitching along marked lines, **Fig 10**.

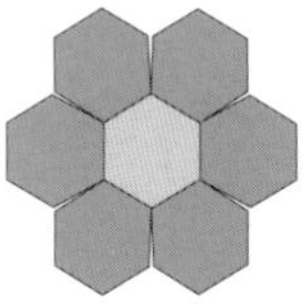
Fig 10

10. Hand piece adjoining sides of hexagons in middle row from center toward outside edge. Then, add outer row of hexagons in same manner, **Fig 11**.

11. Baste or press under seam allowances on outside edges of all Grandmother's Flower Garden blocks and Hexagons to prepare for appliqué. Set aside.

12. Press under 1/4" on long edges of dk brown bias strips for basket rim. Set aside.

13. Make two Grandmother's Flower Garden blocks, **Fig 11**, one half block, **Fig 12** and one block which is missing one hexagon from the outer ring of hexagons, **Fig 13**.

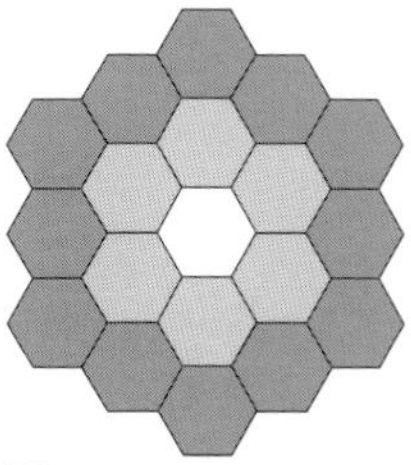
Fig 11

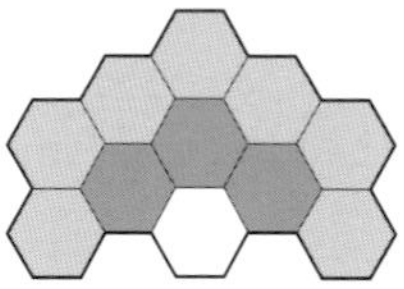
Fig 12

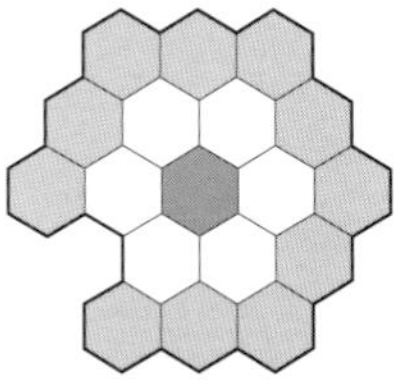
Fig 13

14. Sew a 1 1/2" x 28 1/2" dk print strip to opposite sides of 28 1/2" muslin background square; press toward border strips. Sew 1 1/2" x 30 1/2" dk print strips to top and bottom; press toward border strips.

15. For inner basket, place the 3" x 18" neutral print strip across top edge of basket; trim right short edge at a diagonal even with diagonal edge of basket, **Fig 14**.

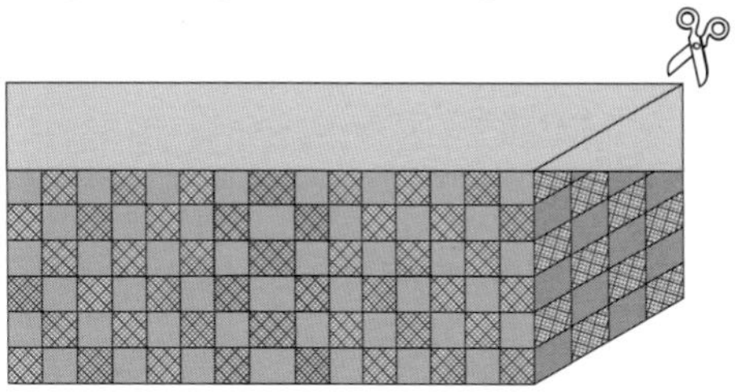
Fig 14

16. Referring to photograph for placement, position basket, inner basket, Front and Back Handles, one complete Grandmother's Flower Garden block and the half Flower Garden block in position in basket. Place bias strips on top of raw edges of basket, **Fig 15**. Adjust pieces as desired until you are happy with the placement of the pieces; baste carefully and completely.

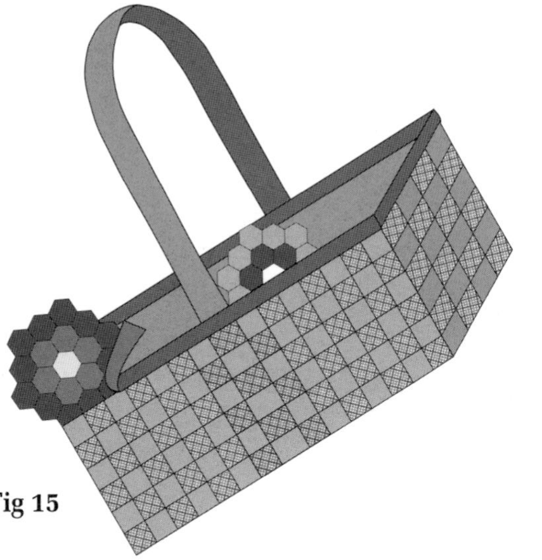

Fig 15

17. Appliqué pieces along pressed edges referring to Basic Appliqué, pages 5 and 6.

Hint: *After appliqué is complete, trim away extra layers of fabric from behind basket and flowers. It is much easier to quilt through one layer of fabric rather than multiple layers.*

18. Referring to photograph, position Scissors Back Blade, Scissors Front Blade, Left and Right Scissors Handles, Appliqué Spool (O and P), Needle, and additional Flower Garden Block and hexagons onto background fabric; appliqué in place. Trim away background fabric if desired.

Sampler Blocks

Note: *You may substitute your own favorite traditional patterns for some of the blocks. Draft your patterns on graph paper so that the finished block is 5 1/2" including outer seam allowances.*

Nine Patch Block

1. Sew dk print square (B) to opposite sides of a lt print square (B), **Fig 16**; repeat. Sew lt print square (B) to opposite sides of dk print square (B), **Fig 17**. Sew rows together to form Nine Patch, **Fig 18**.

Fig 16

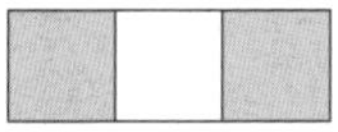

Fig 17

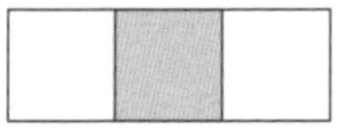

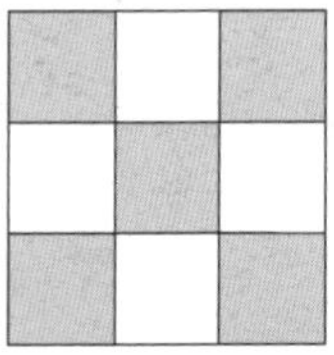

Fig 18

Nine Patch Block

2. Repeat step one for a total of four Nine Patch Blocks.

Appliqué Heart Block

1. Press under edge of Heart.

2. Position Heart in the center of 5 1/2" background square; appliqué referring to Basic Appliqué, pages 5 and 6, **Fig 19**.

3. Repeat steps 1 and 2 for a total of four Appliqué Heart Blocks.

Appliqué Heart Block

Fig 19

Spool Block

1. Sew spool fabric Trapezoids (C) to opposite sides of Spool Square (D), **Fig 20**.

2. Sew background Trapezoids (C) to remaining sides of Square (D), **Fig 21**.

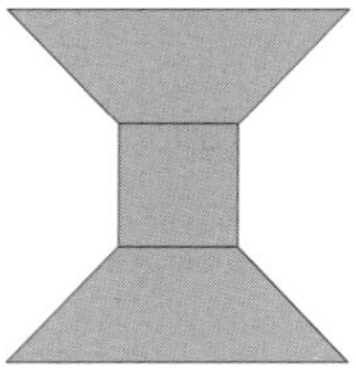

Fig 20

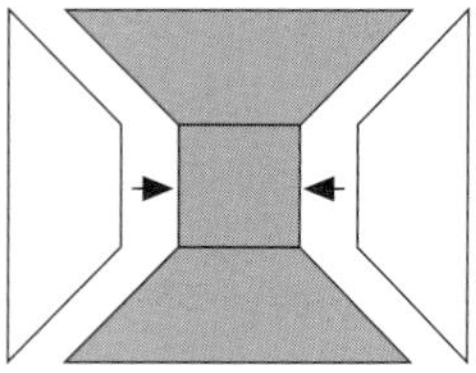

Fig 21

3. Sew diagonal seams of trapezoids starting at inner corner and working toward outside edge, **Fig 22**, to complete Spool Block, **Fig 23**.

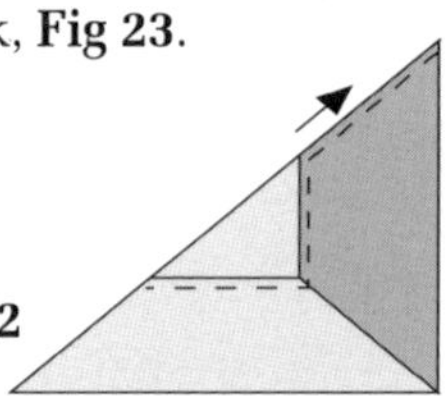

Fig 22

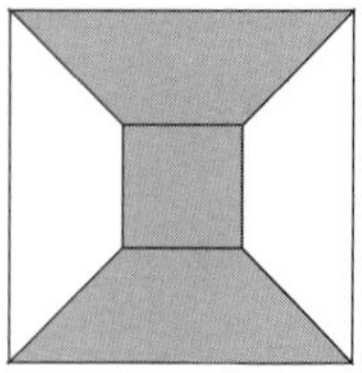

Fig 23

Spool Block

4. Repeat steps 1 to 3 for a total of six Spool Blocks.

Pinwheel Block

1. Sew a light and dark Pinwheel Triangle (E) together along diagonal edge to form a square, **Fig 24**. Repeat three more times.

2. Sew four squares to complete Pinwheel Block, **Fig 25**.

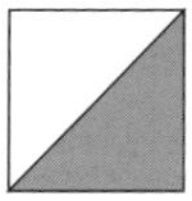

Fig 24

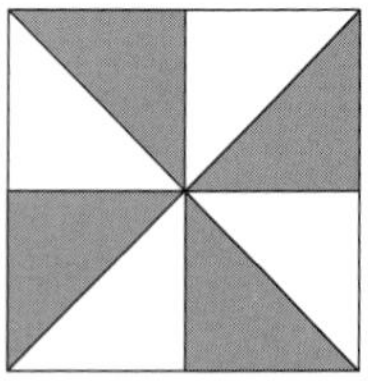

Fig 25

Pinwheel Block

3. Repeat steps 1 and 2 for a total of four Pinwheel Blocks.

Star Block

1. Sew a Small Star Triangle (G) to each short side of Large Star Triangle (H), **Fig 26**; repeat three more times.

2. Sew Small Star Square (F) to opposite sides of unit made in step 1 for row 1, **Fig 27**; repeat for row 3.

Fig 26

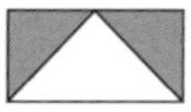

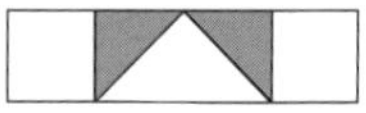

Fig 27

3. Sew remaining units from step 1 to opposite sides of Large Star Square (I), **Fig 28**, for row 2.

4. Sew rows together to form Star Block, **Fig 29**.

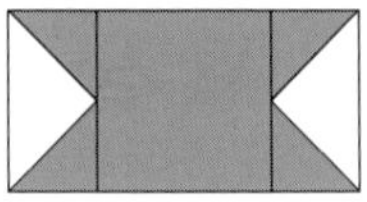

Fig 28

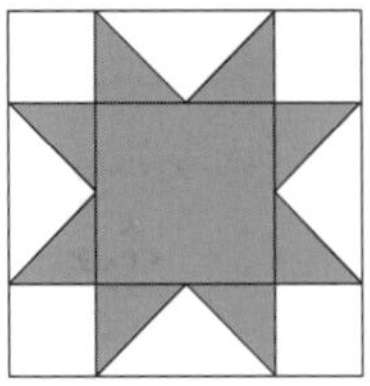

Fig 29

Star Block

5. Repeat steps 1 to 4 for a total of four Star Blocks.

Basket Block

1. Sew background fabric Rectangle (J) to basket fabric Triangle (M), **Fig 30**; repeat.

2. Sew units from step 1 to short sides of basket fabric Triangle (K), **Fig 31**.

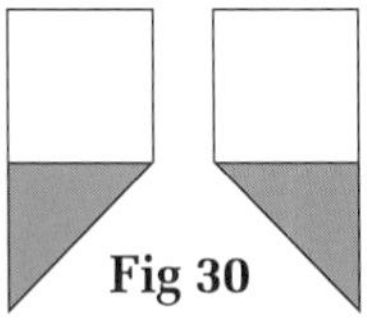

Fig 30

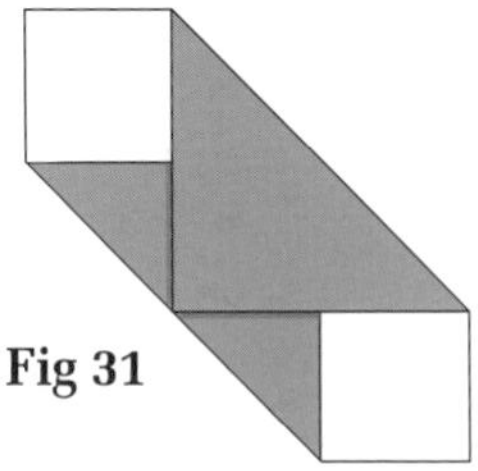

Fig 31

3. Press curved edges of basket fabric Handle (Y) under 1/4" toward wrong side; appliqué to background fabric Triangle (K) following placement on **Fig 32**. Sew Triangle with Handle to Large Basket Triangle, **Fig 33**.

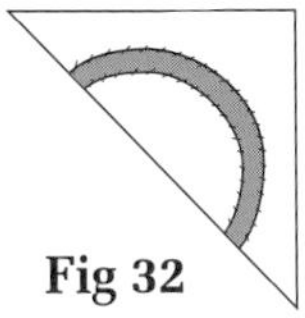

Fig 32

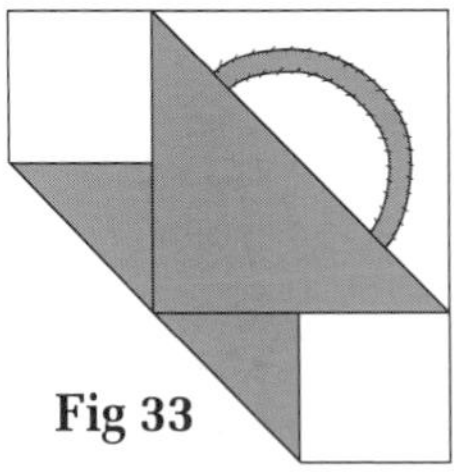

Fig 33

4. Sew background fabric Triangle (L) to lower edge of basket to complete Basket Block, **Fig 34**.

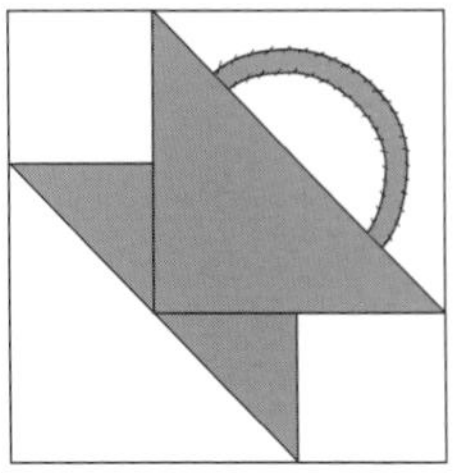

Fig 34

Basket Block

5. Repeat steps 1 to 4 to complete six Basket Blocks.

Finishing

1. Place Sampler Blocks around central portion of quilt. Refer to Layout or place them as desired.

2. Sew six blocks together for each side; sew to sides of quilt.

3. Sew eight blocks together for top and bottom; sew to quilt.

4. For thread in eye of Needle, embroider Outline Stitch using six strands of embroidery floss, **Fig 35**. Repeat for "loose" end of thread from spool.

5. Embroider rim lashing of basket with Couching Stitch, **Fig 36**, following lettering in enlarged diagram.

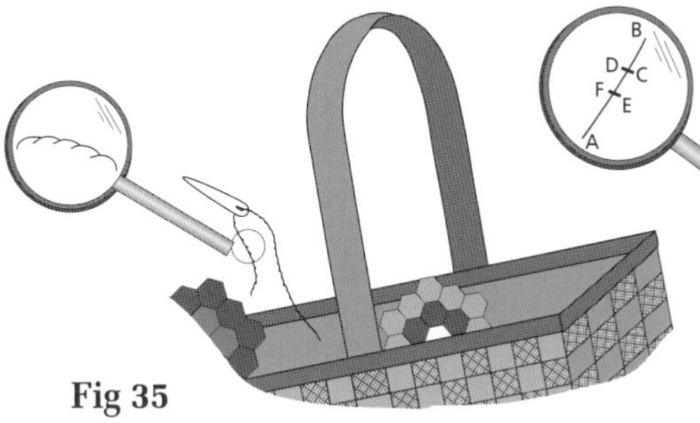

Fig 35

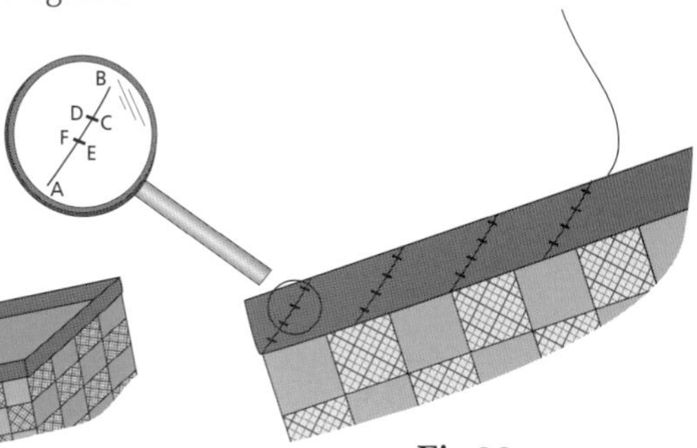
A
B
C
D
E
F

Fig 36

6. Layer backing, batting and quilt top. Baste by hand or with safety pins. Quilt as desired. Photographed quilt was hand quilted as follows: with dark brown thread on the handles to represent woodgrain and in the ditch in the basket squares to enhance the woven appearance; with white quilting thread for rays coming from the center of the basket to suggest movement, and hexagons in the background fabric to carry the Grandmother's Flower Garden effect further; and finally, outline and free form quilting in the sampler blocks.

7. See Attaching the Binding, page 7, to finish quilt.

Quilt Layout

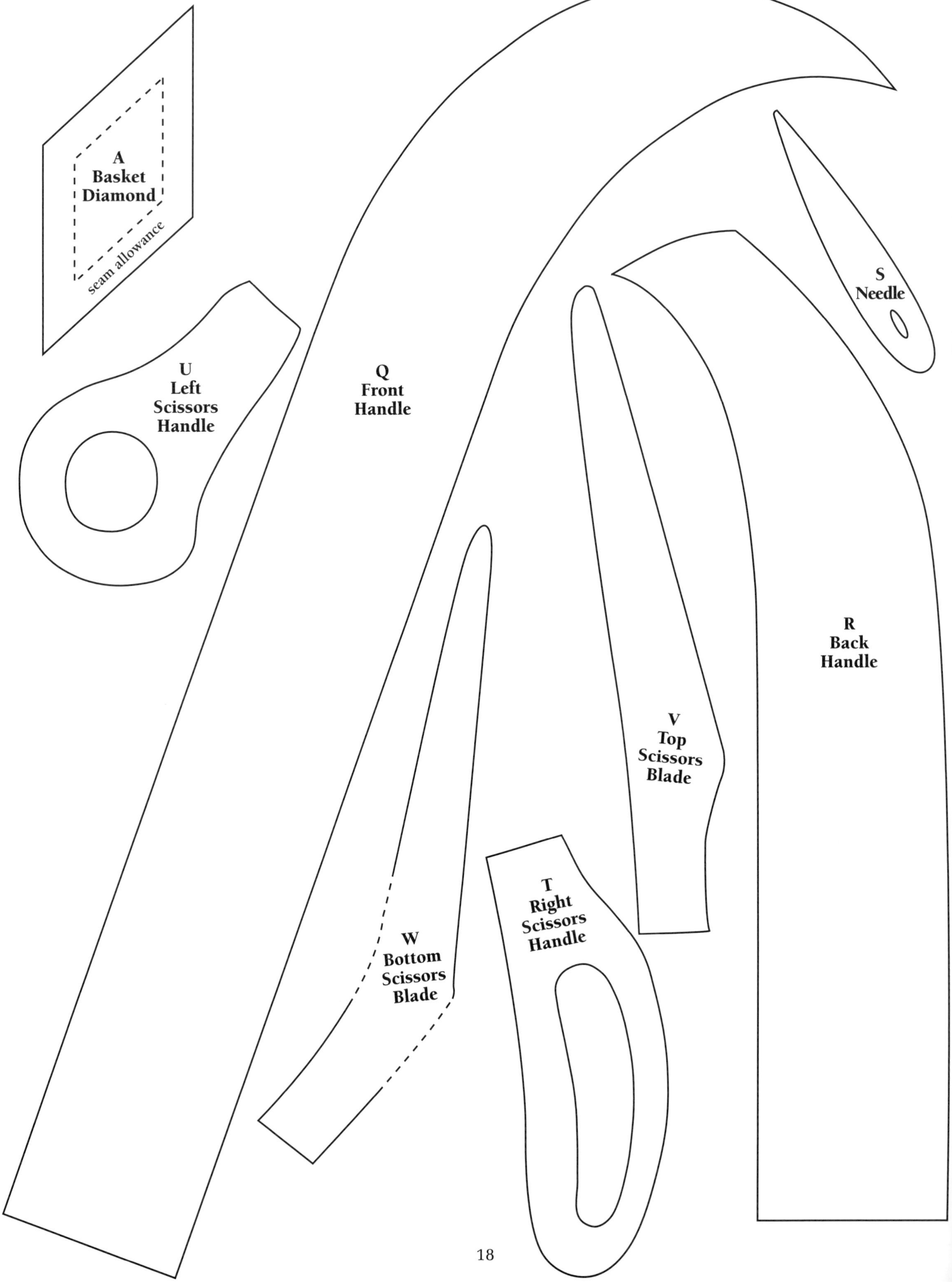
A
Basket
Diamond
seam allowance
U
Left
Scissors
Handle
Q
Front
Handle
S
Needle
R
Back
Handle
V
Top
Scissors
Blade
W
Bottom
Scissors
Blade
T
Right
Scissors
Handle

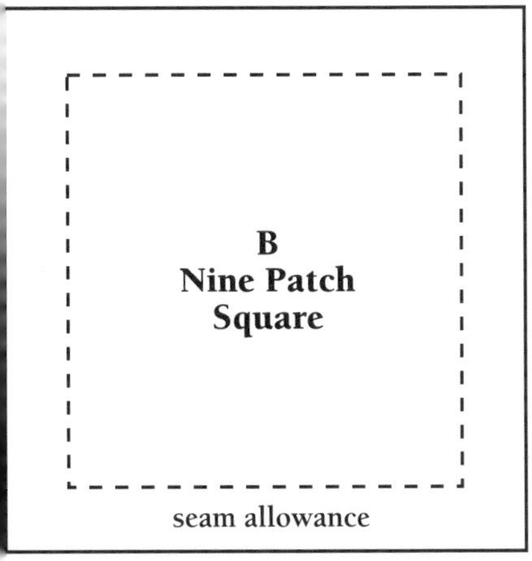
B
Nine Patch
Square
seam allowance

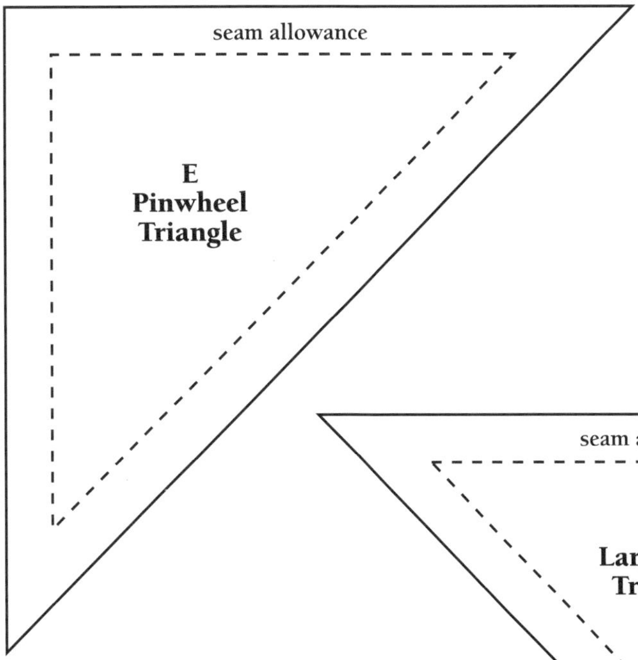
seam allowance
E
Pinwheel
Triangle

F
Small Star
Square
seam allowance

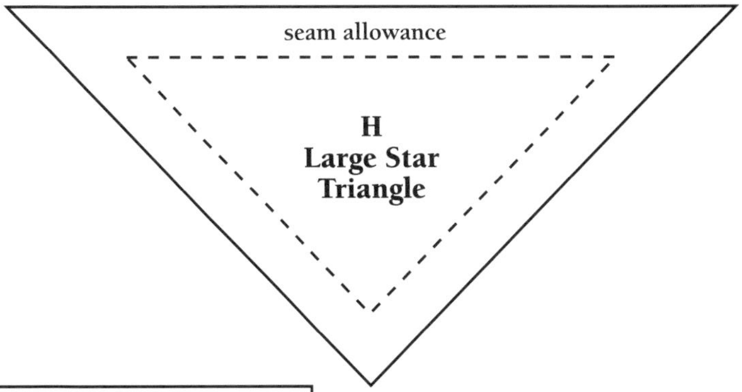
seam allowance
H
Large Star
Triangle

I
Large Star
Square
seam allowance

D
Spool
Square
seam allowance

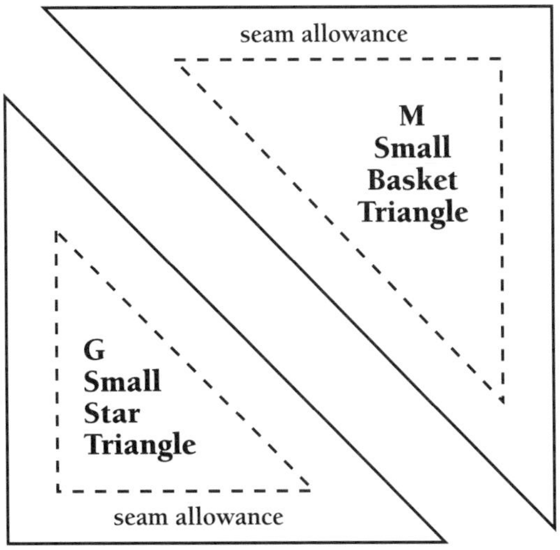
seam allowance
M
Small
Basket
Triangle
G
Small
Star
Triangle
seam allowance

X
Appliqué Heart

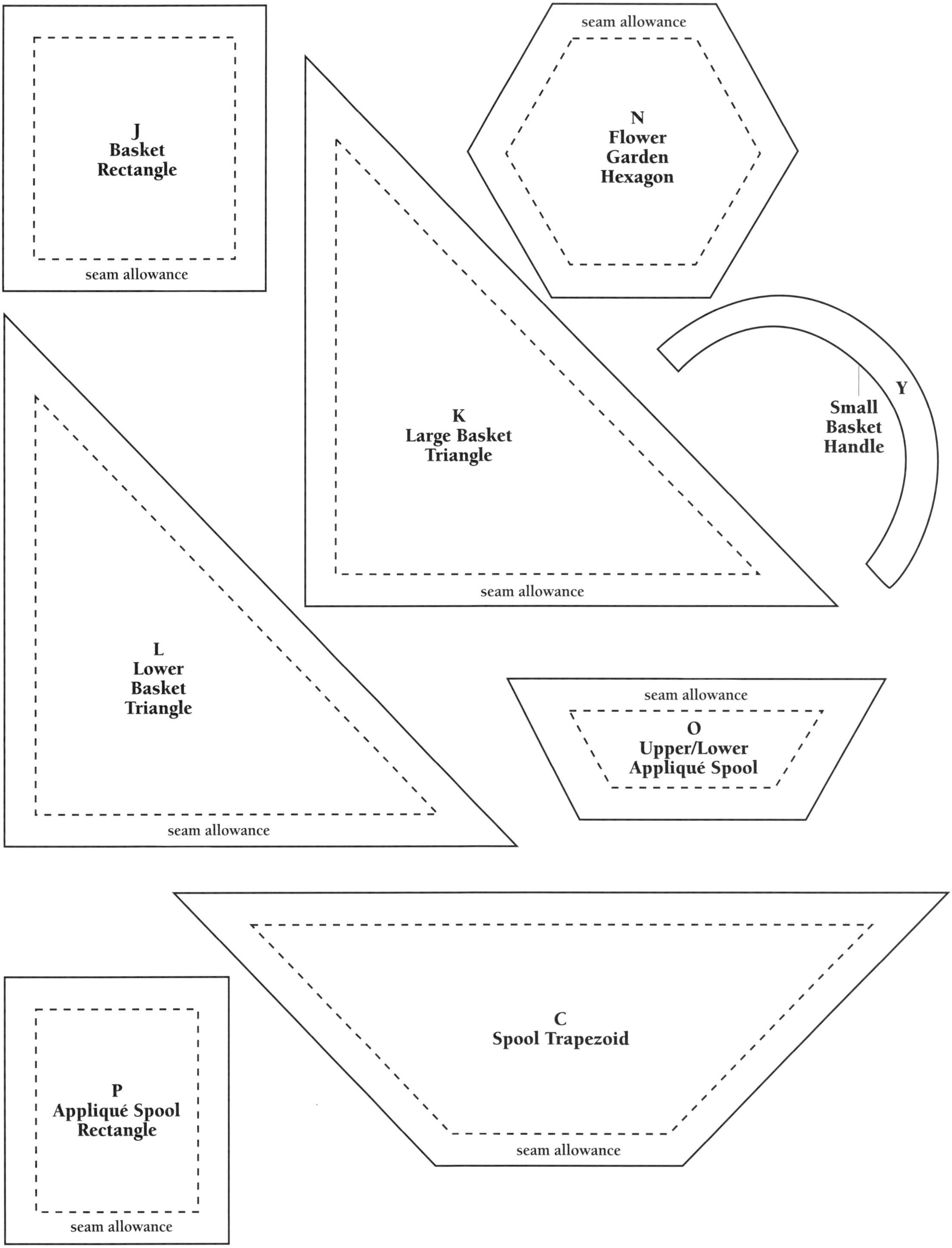
J
Basket
Rectangle
seam allowance
seam allowance
N
Flower
Garden
Hexagon
K
Large Basket
Triangle
seam allowance
Y
Small
Basket
Handle
L
Lower
Basket
Triangle
seam allowance
seam allowance
O
Upper/Lower
Appliqué Spool
C
Spool Trapezoid
seam allowance
P
Appliqué Spool
Rectangle
seam allowance

Jeannie's Summer Basket

by Shirley Kraus
Second Prize
Approximate Size: 35" x 37 1/2"
(without Prairie Points)

"This quilt is dedicated to my daughter who is an avid gardener. It is an original adaptation of the Baltimore Baskets found in quilts in the mid 1800s. The oval setting was used to give the quilt an old-fashioned look. The flowers, leaves and birds were cut from beautiful tropical prints."

Fabric Requirements:

1/2 yd med blue (bias strips for basket)
1 1/4 yds dk print (outside border)
1 yd med pink solid (inside border and border bias strips)
3/4 yd muslin (center oval)
assorted scraps multi-color tropical fabric* or colored fabric as follows:
blues, purples, reds/greens (birds, rose, berries, bluebells); greens (leaves); pinks (folded rosebuds, daisies, flower petals and yellows (roses); reds, pinks (berries, bleeding hearts, rose buds); blues, whites (gathered flowers); yellows (gathered flowers and birds' beaks); and mauves, pinks (bow)
1 1/4 yds (backing)
1/2 yd dk pink (prairie points)

**Placement of pattern pieces on a colorful tropical print can give wonderful effects. Look at the color photograph on page 42. The small pink rosebuds on the lower right of the basket may look like two separate pieces, but they are really leaves (J4) that are placed strategically on the fabric to give the appearance of rosebuds. Also, note the tops of the birds' heads. The bird patterns (D1 and E1) were placed on the fabric so that the very tops of the heads were on a red portion of the fabric giving the birds a two-color appearance.*

Other Supplies:

2/3 yd 1/2" to 5/8"-wide satin ribbon
2 1/2 yds 1/2"-wide flat lace
(trim around edge of center oval)
Optional: white seed beads
(about 225 beads for lace trim)
tracing paper
dark marking pen
marking pencil
embroidery floss,
yellow, med green, dk blue, yellow green, and gray
small amount of polyester stuffing
4 1/2" x 18" piece paper-backed fusible web
Optional: medium blue acrylic paint and a small stiff paint brush

Pattern Pieces (pages 27 to 31):

A Frame 1, 2, 3, 4
B Basket Shape
C Large Bird 1, 2, 3, 4
D Small Bird 1, 2, 3, 4
E Medium Bird 1, 2, 3, 4
F Rose 1, 2, 3, 4, 5, 6, 7, 8, 9, 10
G Bow 1, 2, 3, 4, 5, 6, 7, 8, 9, 10, 11, 12, 13
H Heart 1, 2, 3, 4, 5
I Berries 1, 2, 3
J Leaves 1, 2, 3, 4
K Flower Petal
L Calyxes 1, 2, 3, 4
M Circle (2")
N Circle (2 1/2")
O Circle (4 1/4")
P Circle (1 1/2")
Q Circle (1")

Cutting Requirements:

1. Cut the following border bias strips:
   two 7/8" x 25" bias strips, med pink solid
   two 7/8" x 27" bias strips, med pink solid
2. Cut 66 squares, 2 1/2" x 2 1/2", dk pink solid
3. Cut the following Basket pieces:
   one 1" x 20" bias strip, med blue solid (basket handle)
   nineteen 3/4" x 9" bias strips, med blue solid (basket)
   one 1" x 13" bias strip for basket rim, med blue solid
   one 1" x 7" bias strip for basket base, med blue solid
4. Cut one each of the following Bow pieces (G):
   Bow 1, 2, 4, 7, 10, 11, light pink/mauve
   Bow 3, 5, 6, 8, 9, 12, 13, dark mauve/pink

Shown in color on page 42

5. Cut one each of the following Bird pieces (C, D, E):
   Small Bird 1, 2, 3, blue/purple/red
   Small bird 4, yellow
   Medium Bird 1, 2, 3, blue/purple/red
   Medium Bird 4, yellow
   Large Bird 1, 2, 3, 4, blue/purple/green
   Large Bird (reversed pieces) 1, 2, 3, 4, blue/purple/green
6. Cut one each of the following Rose pieces: (F)
   Rose 1 to 10, red/pink
   Rose 1 to 10, yellow/pink
7. Cut the following Hearts (H):
   nine Heart 1, red
   five Heart 2, red
   one Heart 3, red
   one Heart 4, red
   three Heart 5, red
8. Cut the following Berries (I):
   fifteen Berry 1, red/pink
   seven Berry 1, blue/purple
   eight Berry 2, red/pink
   two Berry 2, blue/purple
   one Berry 3, red/pink
9. Cut the following Leaves (J):
   ten Leaf 1, green
   ten Leaf 2, green
   eleven Leaf 3, green
   six Leaf 4, green/pink
10. Cut the following Calyxes (L):
   two Calyx 1, green
   four Calyx 2, green
   two Calyx 3, green
   one Calyx 4, green

Instructions

Flowers

Large Daisy

1. Cut strip of fabric 2 1/2" x 7"; cut strip of coordinating or contrasting fabric 2" x 7"; cut strip of paper-backed fusible web 2" x 7".

2. Following manufacturer's instructions, iron fusible web to wrong side of 2" x 7" fabric strip; remove paper backing. Center fabric wrong sides together on 2 1/2" x 7" strip, **Fig 1**.

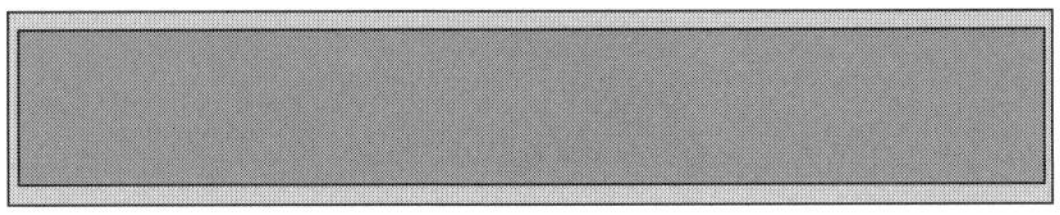

Fig 1

3. Fold strip in half with small strip inside, **Fig 2**. Sew a running stitch 1/8" from raw edge through both outer layers; do not cut thread, **Fig 3**. Cut narrow slits from fold to stitching about 1/16" to 1/8" apart, **Fig 4**.

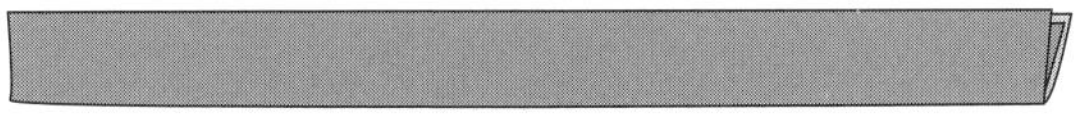

Fig 2

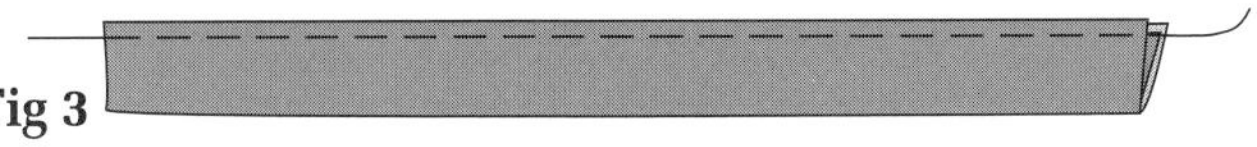

Fig 3

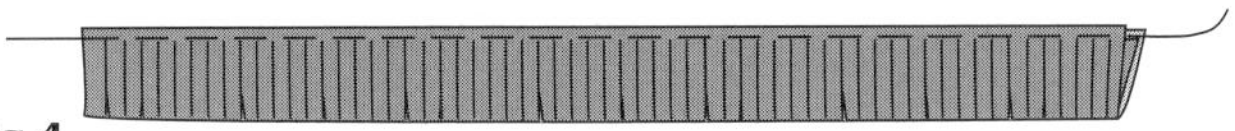

Fig 4

4. Pull thread to gather; tack ends together to form circle, **Fig 5**.

Small Daisy

1. Cut strip of fabric 1 1/4" x 3 1/2"; cut strip of coordinating or contrasting fabric 3/4" x 3 1/2"; cut strip of paper-backed fusible web 3/4" x 3 1/2".

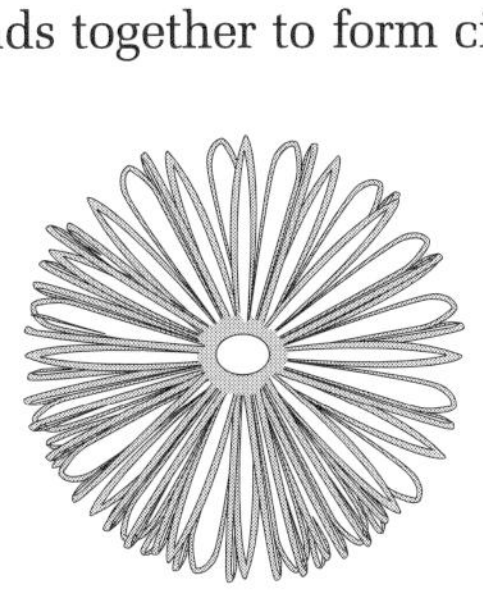

Fig 5

2. Repeat steps 2 to 4 of Large Daisy to complete Small Daisy.

Bluebells

1. Cut 2 1/2" circle from fabric.

***Note:** For a slightly smaller flower, use a 2 1/4" circle.*

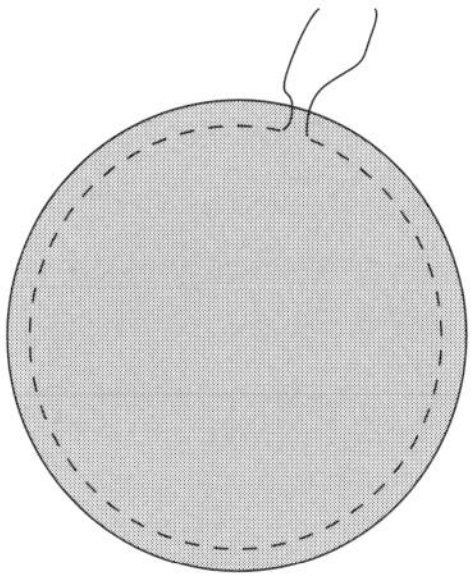

Fig 6

2. Sew running stitch about 1/8" to 1/4" from raw edge, **Fig 6**.

3. Pull thread to gather to form bell shape, **Fig 7**; knot end.

4. Lightly rub raw edges to fray ends.

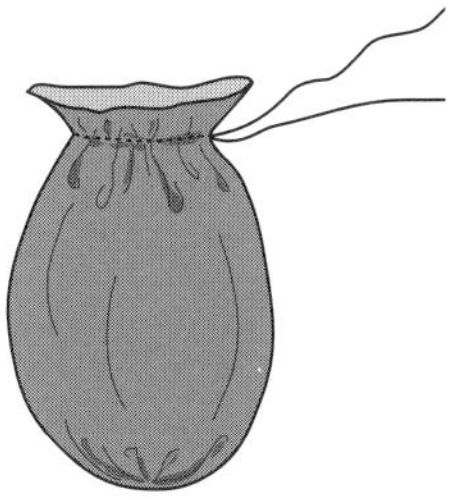

Fig 7

Yo-Yo Flowers

1. Cut a 2"-diameter circle from fabric.

2. Place a tiny bit of polyester stuffing in center of circle (on wrong side); sew a gathering stitch in center of circle around stuffing, **Fig 8**. Pull thread to enclose stuffing, **Fig 9**; knot ends.

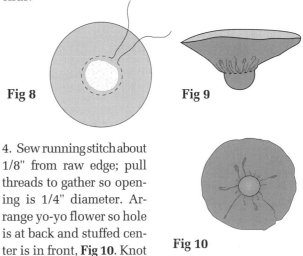

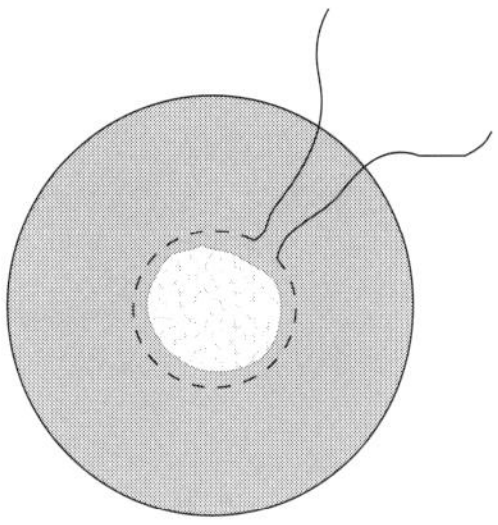

Fig 8

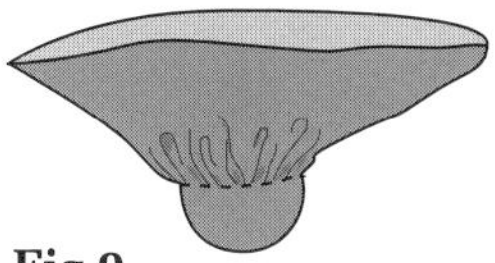

Fig 9

4. Sew running stitch about 1/8" from raw edge; pull threads to gather so opening is 1/4" diameter. Arrange yo-yo flower so hole is at back and stuffed center is in front, **Fig 10**. Knot ends.

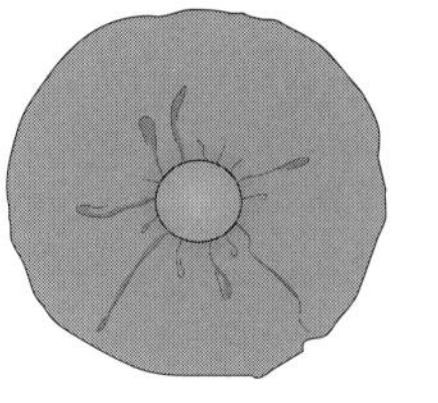

Fig 10

Gathered Flowers

1. Cut a 4 1/4" circle from fabric.

2. Fold under raw edge 3/8"; sew running stitch in a scallop pattern, **Fig 11**. Do not cut or pull threads at this time.

3. Using a new length of thread, sew running stitch in a spiral pattern in center of circle, leaving a tail on both ends, **Fig 12**.

4. Pull all thread ends to gather into pleasing shape, **Fig 13**; knot ends.

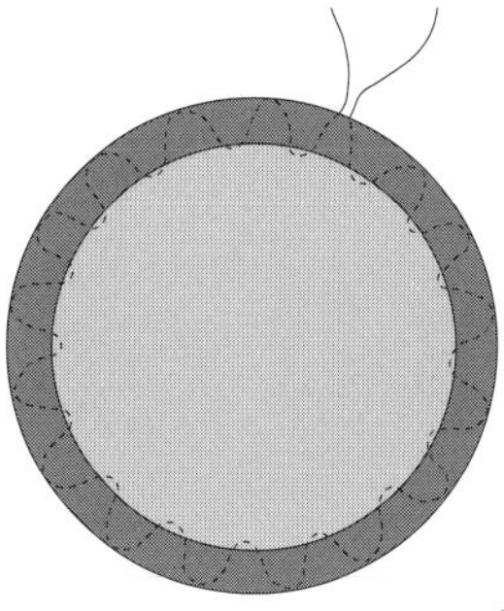

Fig 11

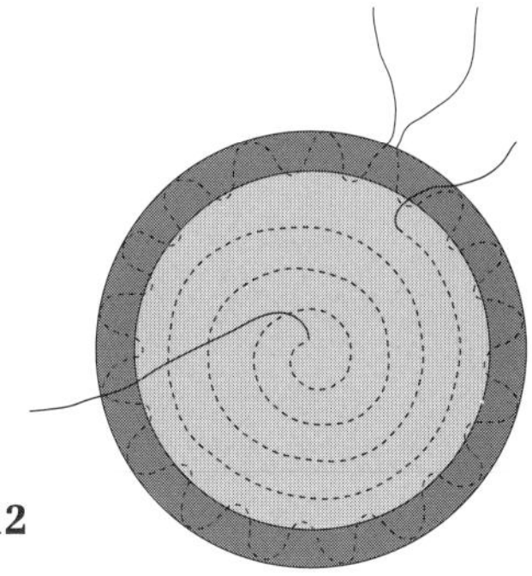

Fig 12

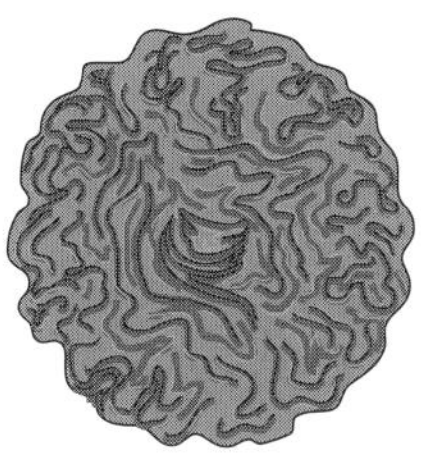

Fig 13

Ribbon Flowers

1. Cut 12" length of 1/2" to 5/8"-wide ribbon.

2. Starting about 1" from one end, sew a small running stitch at a 45 degree angle; go back down at a 45 degree angle. Continue stitching in this manner, **Fig 14**, to about 1" from opposite end of ribbon.

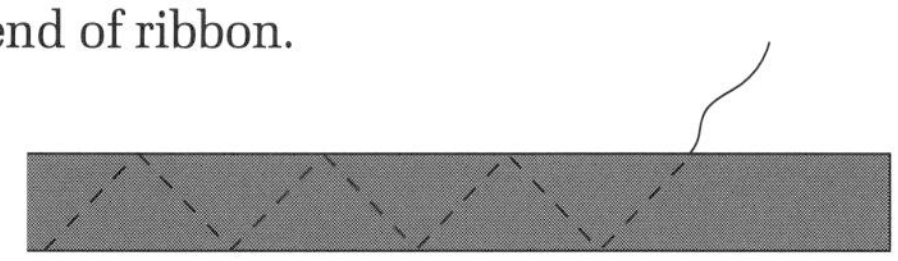

Fig 14

3. Pull thread to gather, forming gentle loops; tack ends together to form circle, **Fig 15**.

Fig 15

Folded Rosebuds

1. Cut 1 1/2" diameter circle from fabric.
Note: *For smaller bud, use 1" diameter circle.*

2. Fold circle in half with wrong sides together; fold both sides down to form bud, **Fig 16**.

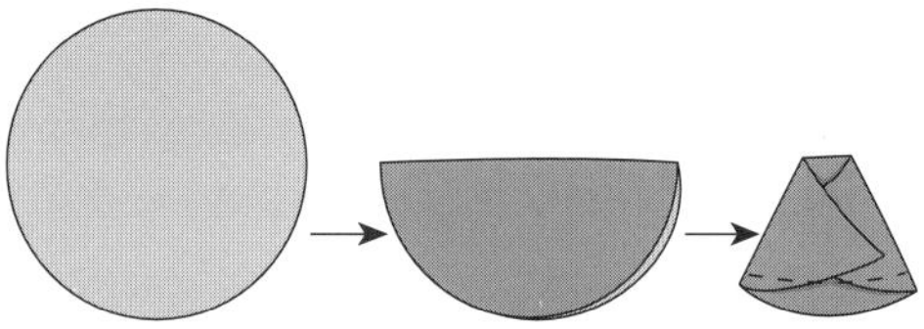

Fig 16

3. Sew gathering stitch about 1/4" from bottom edge; pull thread to gather, **Fig 17**.

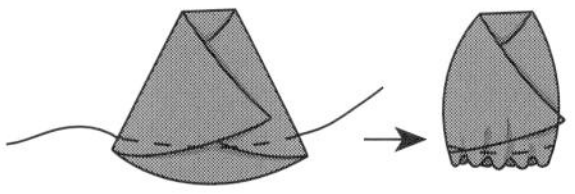

Fig 17

Center Oval Section

Preparing the Oval

1. Trace Frame pattern A onto tracing paper matching notches as indicated on pattern pieces A1, A2, A3 and A4. Note that inner line is for oval shape and outer line is for outer edge of frame. Cut out oval along drawn line.

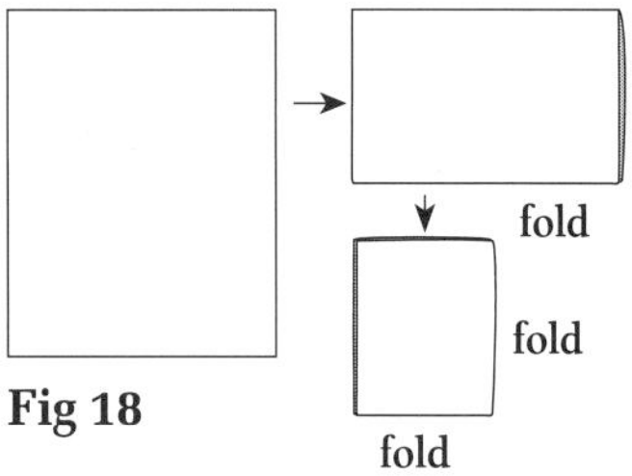
fold
fold
fold

Fig 18

2. Cut a 21 1/2" x 25 1/2" rectangle from muslin. Fold rectangle in half, then in half again, **Fig 18**.

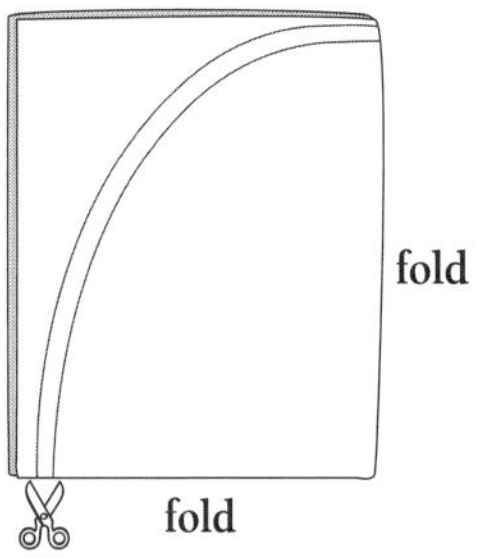
fold
fold

Fig 19

3. Using oval edge of pattern, draw oval shape onto folded muslin; cut 1/4" outside of drawn line, **Fig 19**.

4. Referring to Basket Shape Pattern (B), draw basket design on right side of oval. Draw right half, then flop pattern to draw left half.

5. Appliqué the two horizontal basket strips first, **Fig 20**. Appliqué nineteen med blue bias strips evenly spaced following outer curve of basket, **Fig 21**. Appliqué Basket Handle, Basket Base and Basket Rim.

Fig 20

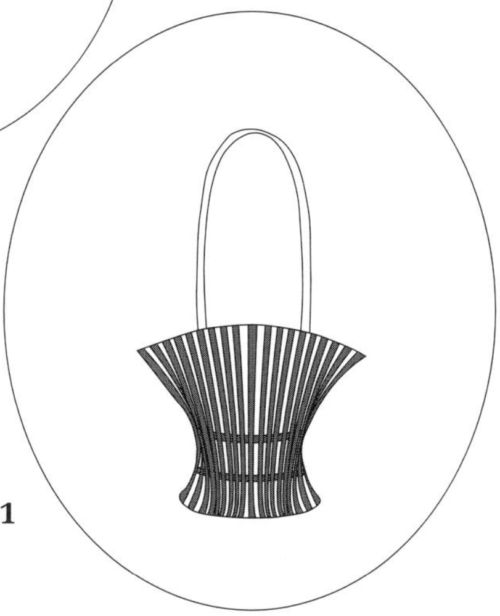

Fig 21

5. To achieve the shading in the basket, the designer painted in between the appliquéd strips. If you would like to have the same effect in your basket, here are the instructions to do this. Dilute paint with water (about one part paint to one part water). Starting at the bottom of the basket, paint in between bias strips being careful not to get paint on the bias strips. To duplicate shading of basket, refer to color photograph and apply more coats of paint at the base, working upwards until desired effect is achieved. Let paint dry thoroughly before continuing.

Appliquéing the Flowers

Note: *Refer to Flower Placement Diagram, page 27, as you appliqué each flower.*

1. Appliqué green bias strips for stems first; then appliqué leaves.

2. Appliqué the two large roses in numerical order according to pattern pieces. Place a pinch of stuffing under each piece as you appliqué for added dimension.
Note: *Do not fold under edges that will be covered by another piece.*

3. Make two Folded Rosebuds (page 24) from 1 1/2" circles of pink fabric and two of red fabric. Make two Folded Rosebuds from 1" circle of red fabric.

Appliqué in place. Appliqué Rosebud Calyxes in place on top of Rosebuds. Appliqué Rosebud Petals on top of Folded Rosebud under Small Bird.

4. Appliqué all leaves.

5. Make three Yo-Yo Flowers (page 23); appliqué in place.

6. Make one Large Daisy (page 23) and appliqué in place. Appliqué circle in center of Daisy to cover raw edges. Make one partial Daisy in the same manner, using 2" long strips instead of 7", **Fig 22**; appliqué in place under Large Daisy.

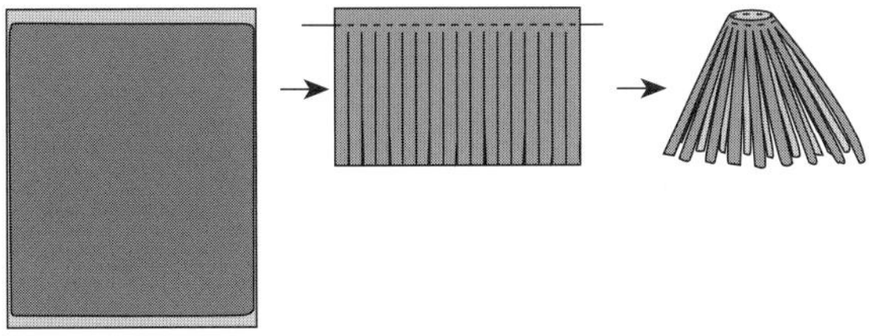

Fig 22

Clip folded ends at an angle for a ragged look, **Fig 23**. Clip top petals about 1/4" shorter to give a two-layered look, **Fig 24**.

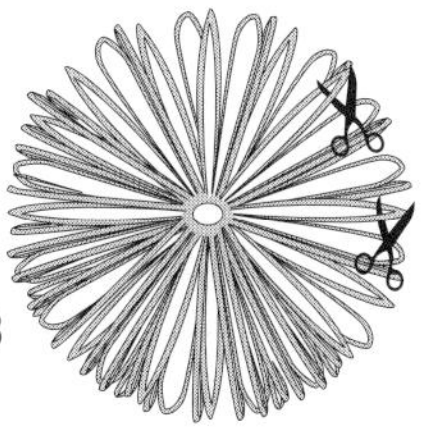

Fig 23

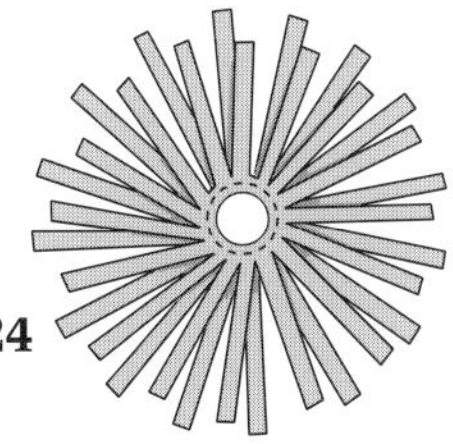

Fig 24

7. Make three Small Daisies (page 23). Appliqué two Daisies in place; appliqué circle in center. Fold one Daisy in half; appliqué in place. Appliqué Calyx (L4) over center of Daisy, **Fig 25**. Make partial Daisies in same manner using 3/4" long, 1" long and 2" long pieces for each. Appliqué in place; appliqué calyxes in place.

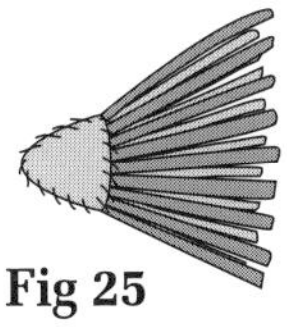

Fig 25

8. Make three Gathered Flowers (page 23); appliqué in place. Embroider small circle in center using med blue embroidery floss and Satin Stitch, **Fig 26**.

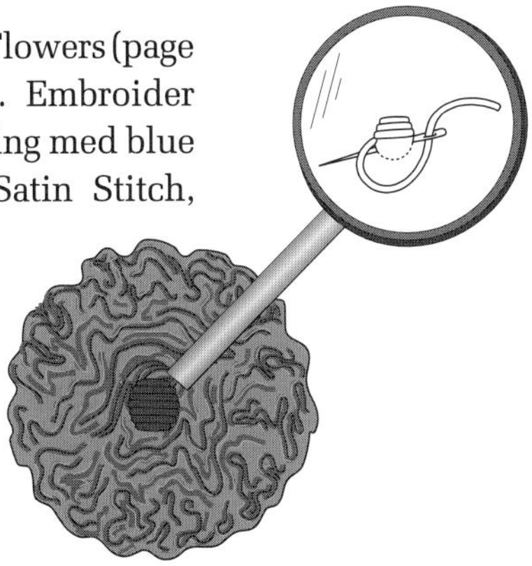

Fig 26

9. Make two Ribbon Flowers (page 24); appliqué in place. Embroider six French Knots in center of flower using yellow embroidery floss, **Fig 27**.

Fig 27

10. Make six Bluebells (page 23); appliqué in place around upper curve of bell shape, leaving frayed edges loose.

11. Appliqué remaining flowers, leaves and birds.

12. Embroider main stems for Bleeding Hearts using green embroidery floss and a Chain Stitch, **Fig 28**. Embroider small individual stems for Bleeding Hearts, stems for Bluebells and veins in leaves using green embroidery floss and Outline Stitch, **Fig 29**.

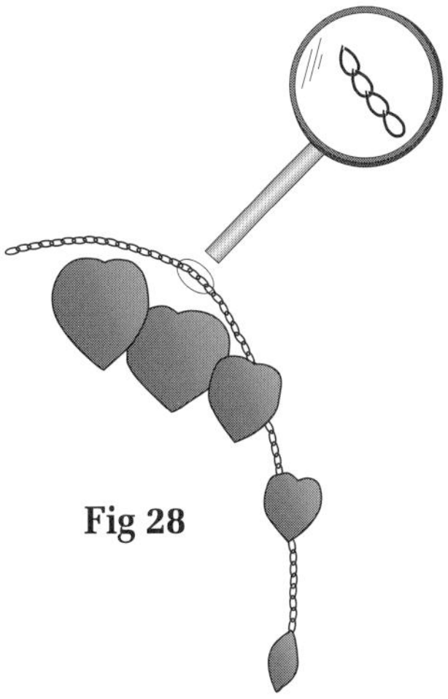

Fig 28

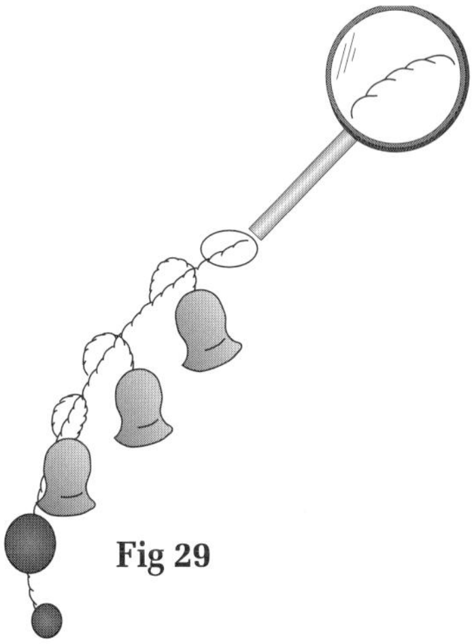

Fig 29

13. Appliqué Bow, following numerical order of pattern pieces, **Fig 30**.

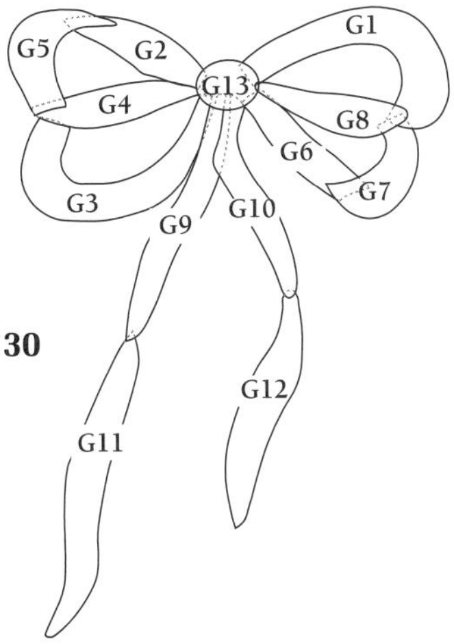
G1
G2
G3
G4
G5
G6
G7
G8
G9
G10
G11
G12
G13

Fig 30

Finishing the Quilt

1. Cut 27 1/2" x 31" rectangle from pink solid. Fold rectangle in half, then in half again (see **Fig 18**). Using outer edge of Frame pattern A, draw outline, **Fig 31**; cut 1/4" outside of drawn line.

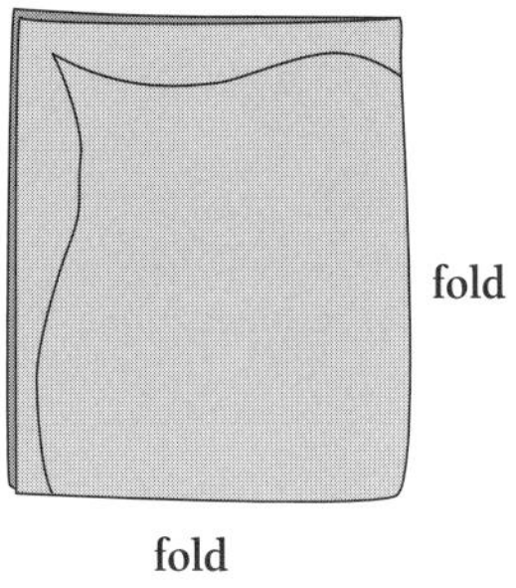
fold
fold

Fig 31

2. Center appliquéd oval on pink fabric; baste in place. Turn edges of oval under 1/4"; hand stitch folded edge.

3. Cover oval seam with flat lace; stitch in place. If desired, sew seed beads at random on lace.

4. Carefully, cut away pink fabric from behind oval to eliminate bulk when quilting.

5. Center pink fabric on top of dk print. Fold edges of pink fabric under 1/4"; appliqué in place.

Quilt Layout

6. For pink border bias strips, fold long raw edges of 7/8" x 27" strip under 1/4"; place 1" from side edge of pink fabric, following curve, **Fig 32**. Appliqué in place. Repeat for opposite edge.

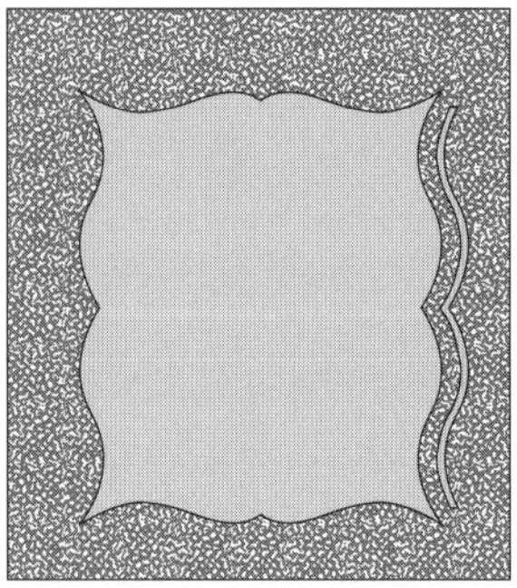

Fig 32

7. Repeat with 7/8" x 25" pink bias strips on top and bottom edges of quilt.

8. Appliqué Large Birds in place at upper corners following numerical sequence of pattern pieces.

9. For prairie points, fold 2" dk pink square in half diagonally with wrong sides together; fold in half again, **Fig 33**. Repeat for a total of 66 squares.

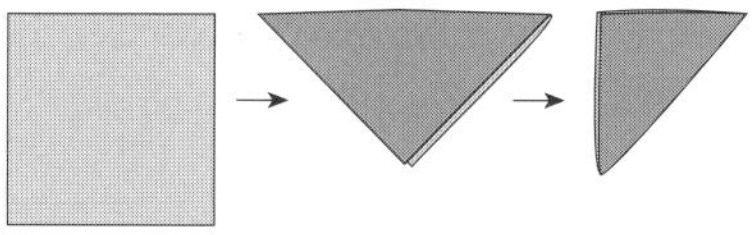

Fig 33

10. Place 33 folded prairie points along one side of quilt (on right side) slipping fold of one prairie point into opening the one next to it, **Fig 34**; adjust as necessary to fit. Machine baste in place 1/4" from raw edge. Repeat on opposite side.

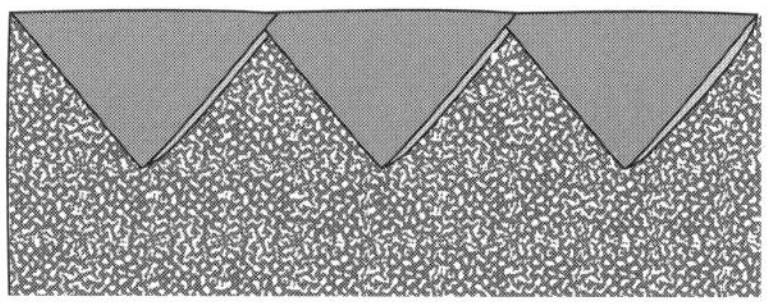

Fig 34

11. Place 30 folded prairie points along top and bottom edges; machine baste in place.

12. Layer backing wrong side up, batting and quilt top right side up; baste layers in place by hand or with safety pins. Quilt as desired.

13. Fold edge of backing under; hand stitch to back of quilt top along stitching line of prairie points.

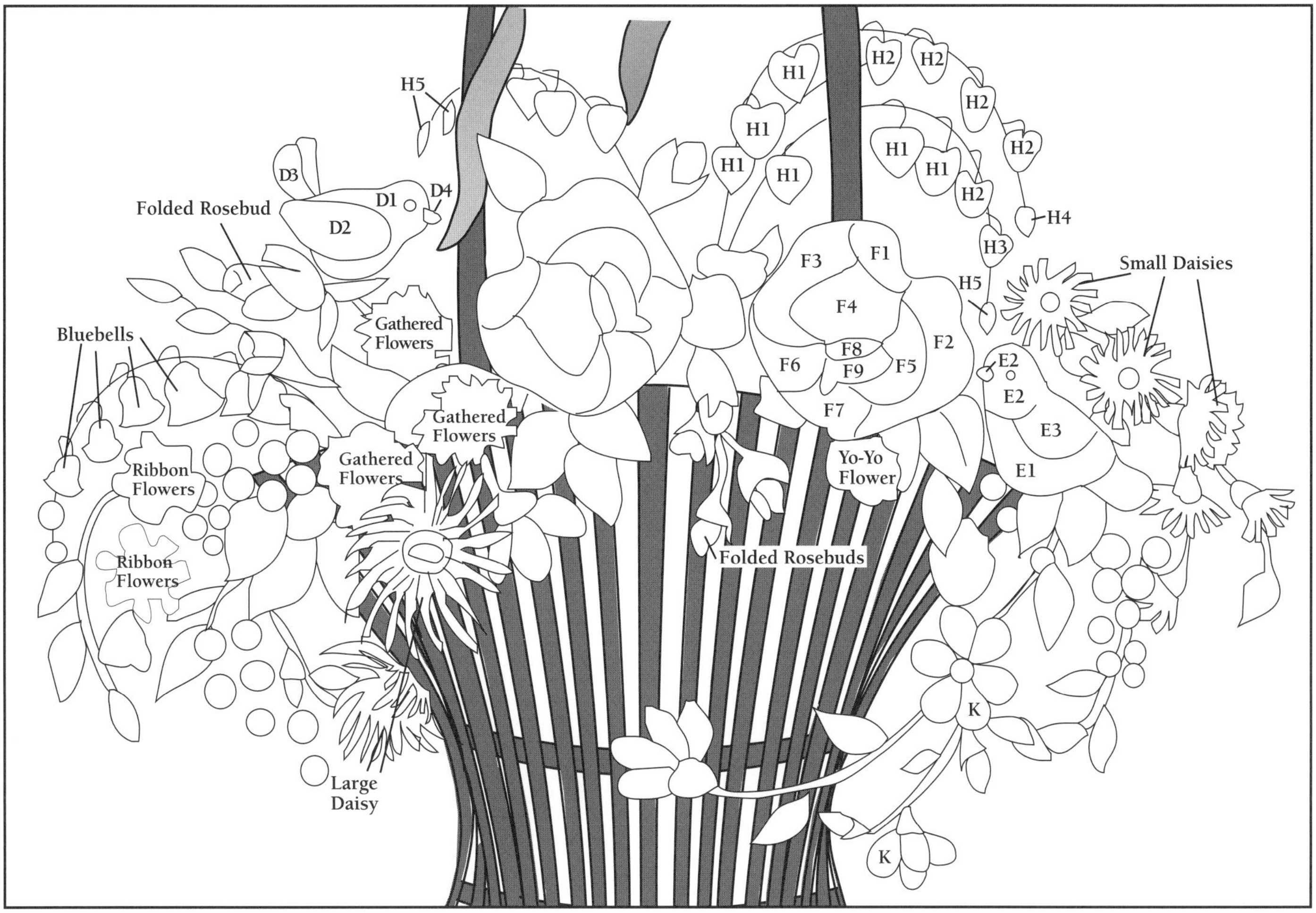
H5
D3
D1
D4
Folded Rosebud
D2
H1
H2
H2
H2
H1
H1
H1
H1
H1
H2
H2
H4
H3
F3
F1
F4
F2
F8
F9
F6
F5
F7
H5
Small Daisies
Bluebells
Gathered Flowers
Gathered Flowers
Gathered Flowers
E2
E2
E3
E1
Ribbon Flowers
Ribbon Flowers
Yo-Yo Flower
Folded Rosebuds
Large Daisy
K
K

Flower Placement Diagram

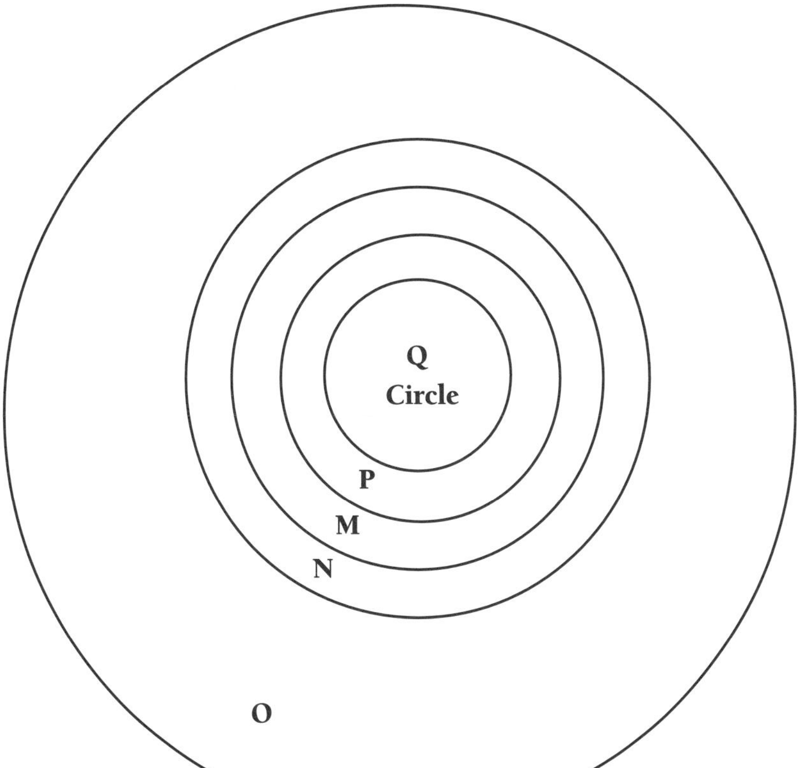
Q
Circle
P
M
N
O

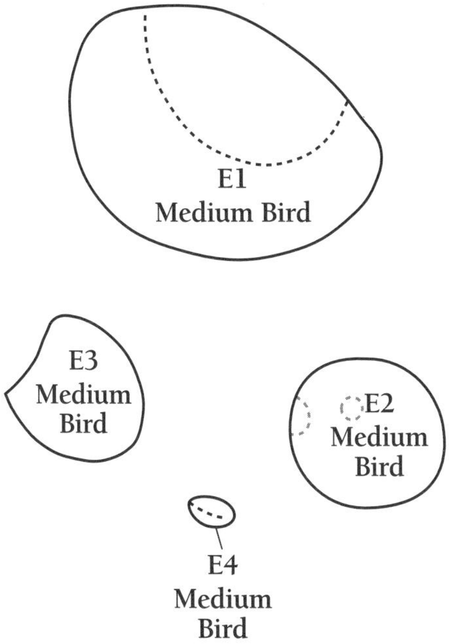
E1
Medium Bird
E3
Medium Bird
E2
Medium Bird
E4
Medium Bird

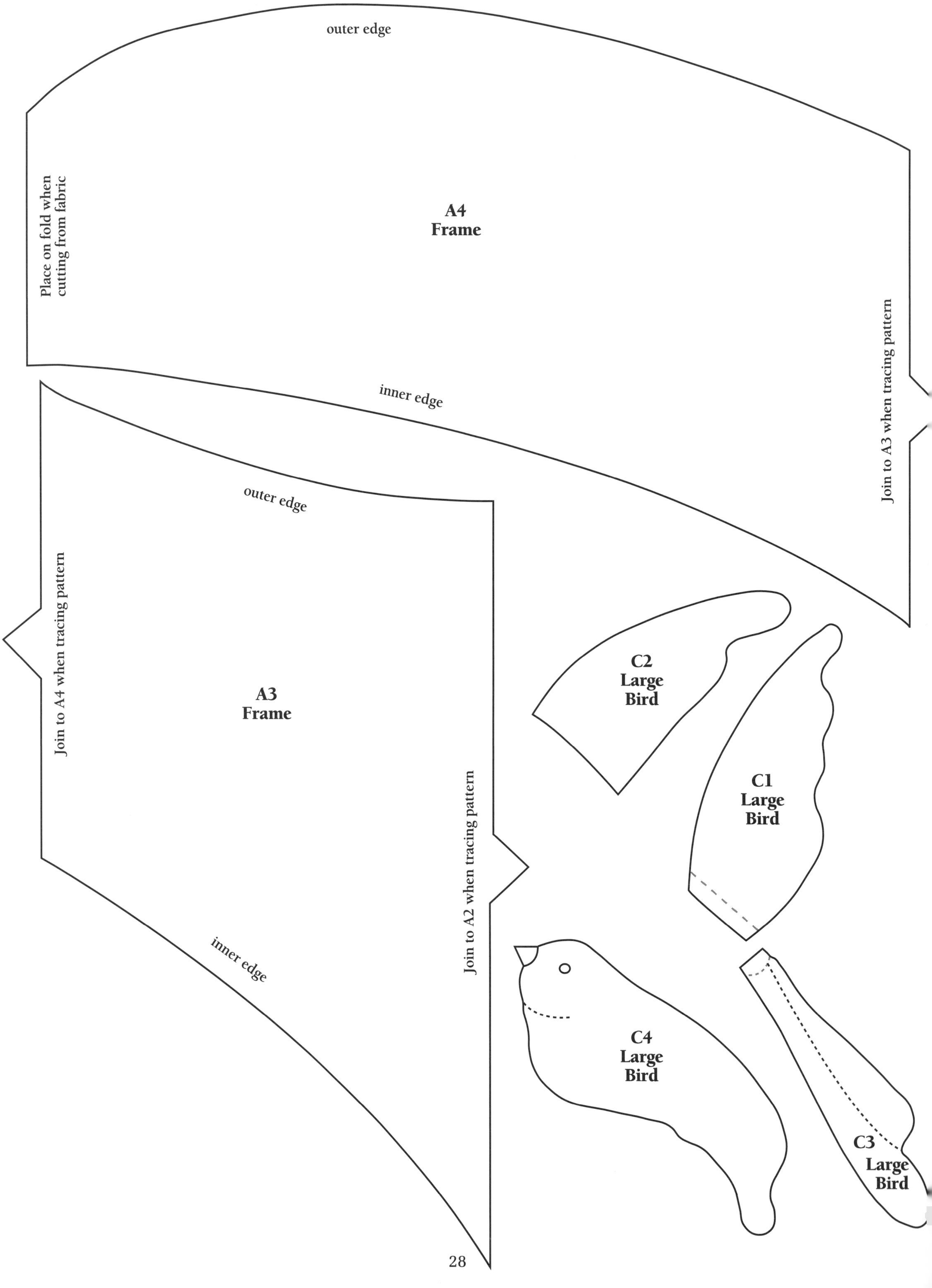
outer edge
A4
Frame
Place on fold when cutting from fabric
Join to A3 when tracing pattern
inner edge
outer edge
A3
Frame
Join to A4 when tracing pattern
Join to A2 when tracing pattern
inner edge
C2
Large
Bird
C1
Large
Bird
C4
Large
Bird
C3
Large
Bird

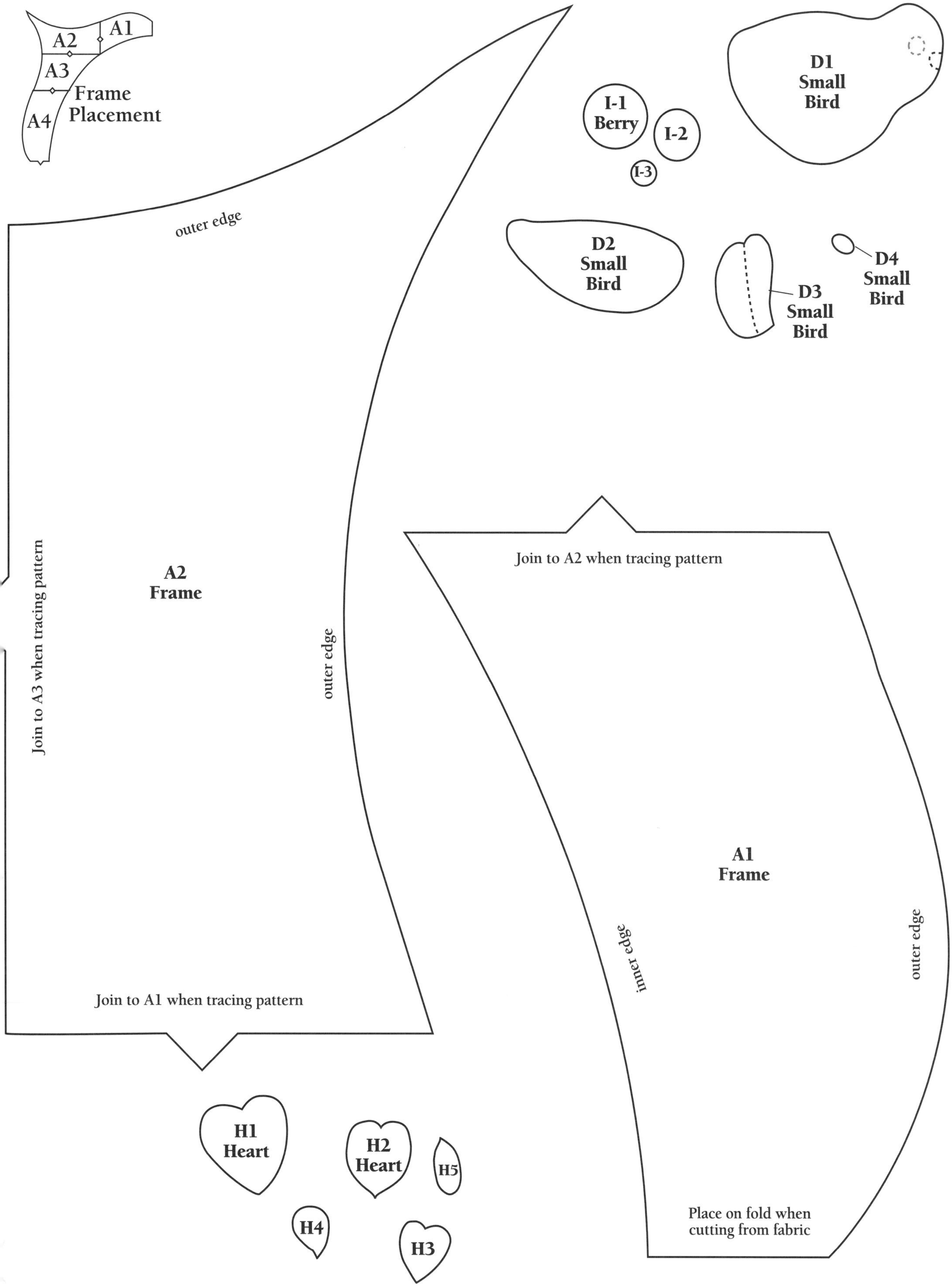
A1
A2
A3
A4
Frame Placement
outer edge
A2 Frame
Join to A3 when tracing pattern
outer edge
Join to A1 when tracing pattern
I-1 Berry
I-2
I-3
D1 Small Bird
D2 Small Bird
D3 Small Bird
D4 Small Bird
Join to A2 when tracing pattern
A1 Frame
inner edge
outer edge
Place on fold when cutting from fabric
H1 Heart
H2 Heart
H3
H4
H5

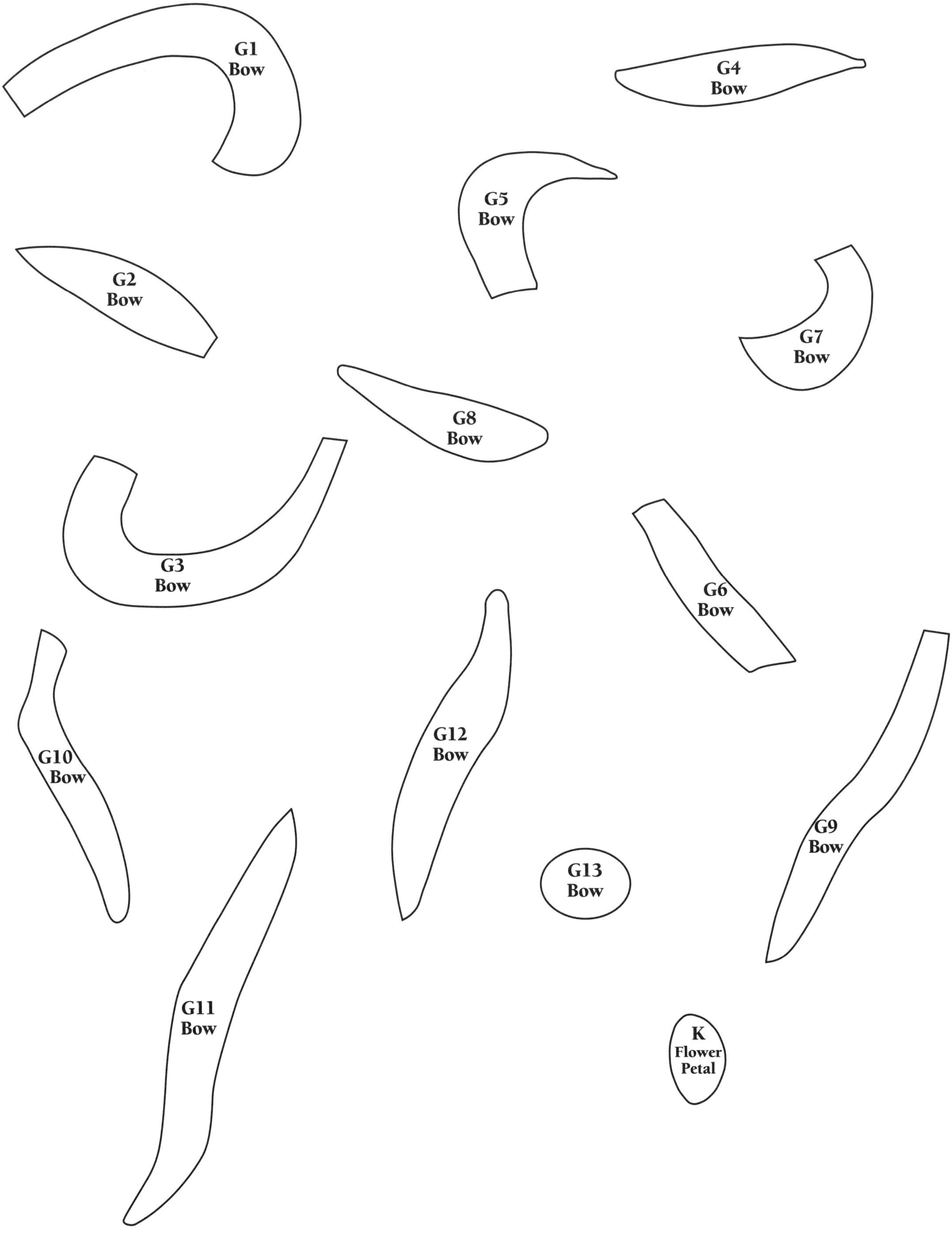
G1
Bow
G4
Bow
G5
Bow
G2
Bow
G7
Bow
G8
Bow
G3
Bow
G6
Bow
G10
Bow
G12
Bow
G9
Bow
G13
Bow
G11
Bow
K
Flower
Petal

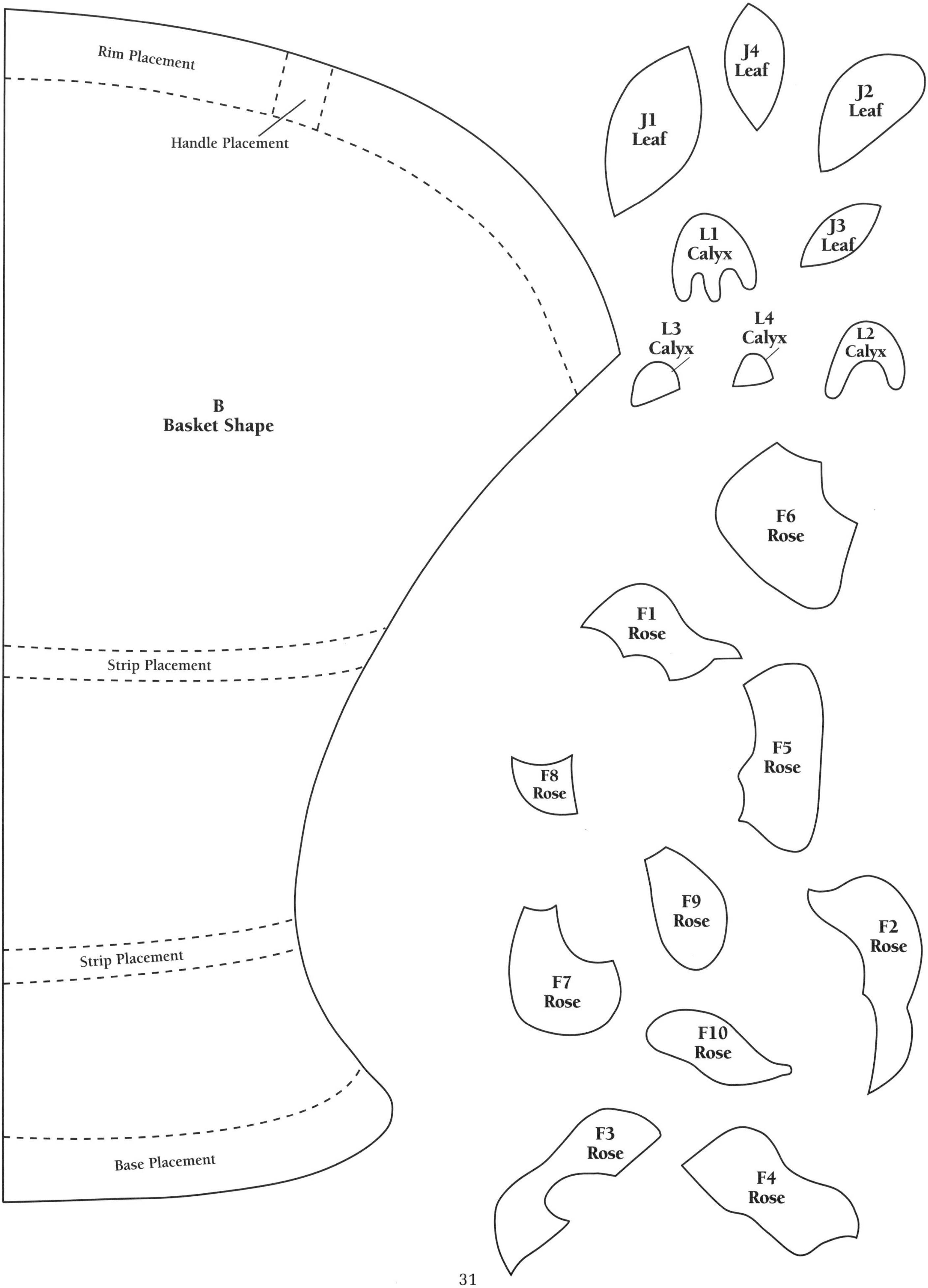
Rim Placement
Handle Placement
B
Basket Shape
Strip Placement
Strip Placement
Base Placement
J4 Leaf
J1 Leaf
J2 Leaf
L1 Calyx
J3 Leaf
L3 Calyx
L4 Calyx
L2 Calyx
F6 Rose
F1 Rose
F5 Rose
F8 Rose
F9 Rose
F2 Rose
F7 Rose
F10 Rose
F3 Rose
F4 Rose

Mae's Baskets

by Nancy Wagner Graves
Third Place
Approximate Size: 40 1/2" x 40 1/2"

"My grandmother, Mae Gourland, made many quilts and was always sewing for me as I was growing up. I believe I learned to love sewing and fabric from her. As I began to think about the quilt contest, I decided to make a very traditional quilt using the colors and patterns my grandmother would have chosen. I used pastels on a white background. The center four blocks are Basket of Lillies *set on point. They are surrounded by an original appliquéd flower bouquet with folded roses and three-dimensional violets with seed beads attaching them. I completed the design with a border of baskets. I made this quilt as a tribute to my grandmother who reached her 90th birthday."*

Fabric Requirements:

1 1/2 yds white solid (background)
1/2 yd pink print (border)
green prints
assorted pastels (border baskets, center flowers, appliqué flowers)
1 1/4 yd backing fabric

Additional Supplies:

purple seed beads

Pattern Pieces (pages 38 to 40):

Center Baskets

A Triangle
B Diamond
C Square
D Triangle
E Triangle
F Rectangle
G Triangle
H Rectangle
I Triangle
J Triangle

Border Baskets

K Rectangle
L Triangle
M Triangle
N Triangle
O Basket Handle

Additional Pieces

P Corner Triangle
Q Border Triangle
R Leaf
S Calyx
T Left Bow Loop
U Center Bow Loop
V Right Bow Loop
W Streamer
X Bow Knot
Y Circle
Z Square

Cutting Requirements:

Center Baskets

Cut the following:

48 Diamonds (B), four each of twelve different pastel prints
twelve Triangles (A), green print
twelve Squares (C), white
24 Triangles (D), white
eight Triangles (E), white
four Rectangles (F), white*
four Triangles (G), green print
eight Rectangles (H), white
eight Triangles (I), white
four 1 1/4" x 9 1/4" bias strips, green print

**Mark stem placement lines on right side of F Rectangles.*

Border Baskets

Cut the following:

64 Rectangles (K), white
32 Triangles (L), white
32 Triangles (M), white
32 Triangles (M), pastel*
64 Triangles (N), pastel*
32 Basket Handles (O), pastel*

**Use same pastel print throughout each individual block.*

Additional Border Pieces

eight Corner Triangles (P), white
60 Border Triangles (Q), white

Shown in color on page 41

Appliqué Pieces

Cut the following:

72 Leaves (R), assorted green prints
sixteen Calyx (S), assorted green prints
four Left Bow Loops (T), blue print*
four Center Bow Loops (U), blue print*
four Right Bow Loops (V), blue print*
eight Streamers (W), blue print *
four Bow Knots (X), blue print*
48 Circles (Y), assorted purple prints
sixteen Squares (Z), pink print
1"-wide bias strips, green print

**Use same blue print throughout each single bow.*

Border and Binding

four 1 3/4" x 44" strips, pink print
four 2 1/2" x 44" strips, pink print

Instructions

Center Baskets

Make four

1. Sew two pastel Diamonds (B) together, **Fig 1**; repeat. Sew pairs together, **Fig 2**.

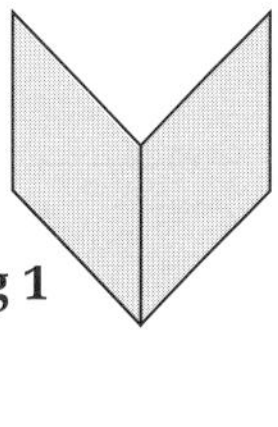

Fig 1

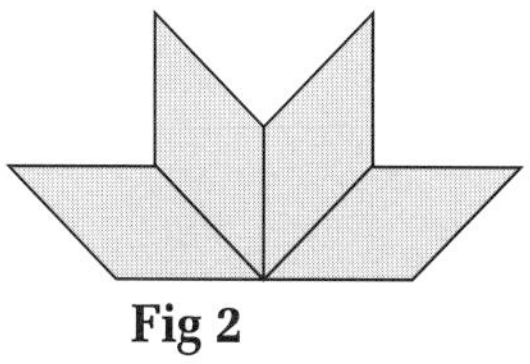

Fig 2

2. Sew green print Triangle (A) to lower edge of diamonds, **Fig 3**.

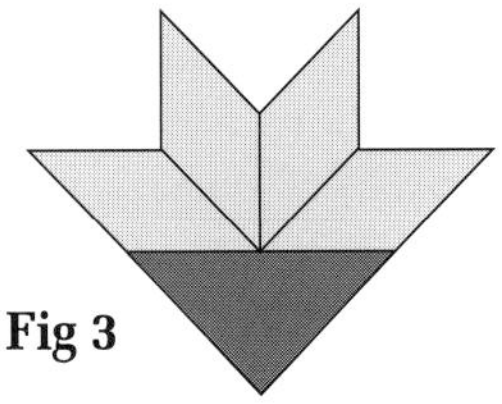

Fig 3

3. Sew a white Triangle (D) in between points of two diamonds in position shown; sew one edge starting from inner corner to outside edge, **Fig 4**. Repeat for adjacent edge, **Fig 5**.

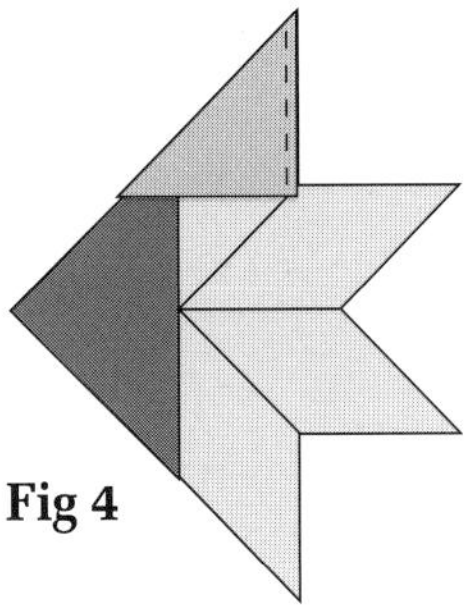

Fig 4

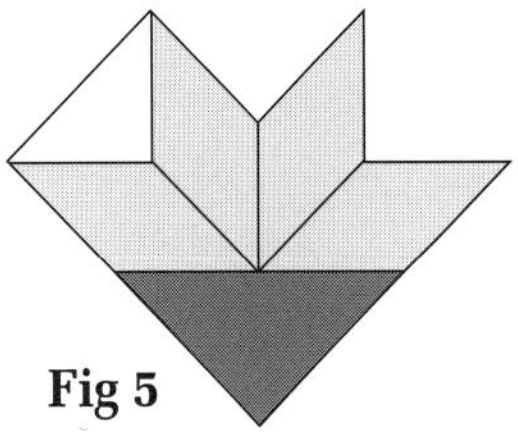

Fig 5

4. Sew another Triangle (D) and a Square (C) between diamonds in same manner as step 3, **Fig 6**.

5. Repeat steps 1 to 4 for two more flowers, positioning the Squares (C) and Triangles (D) as shown, **Fig 7**.

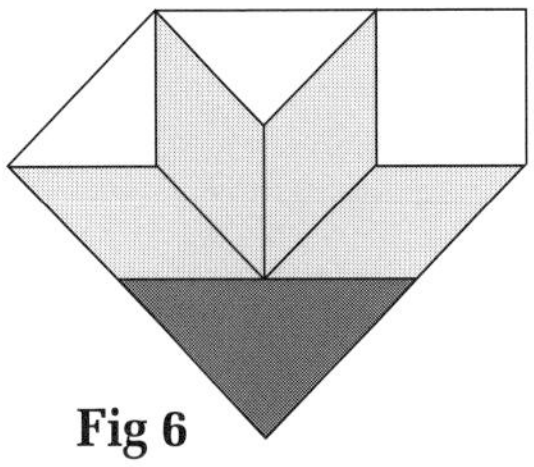

Fig 6

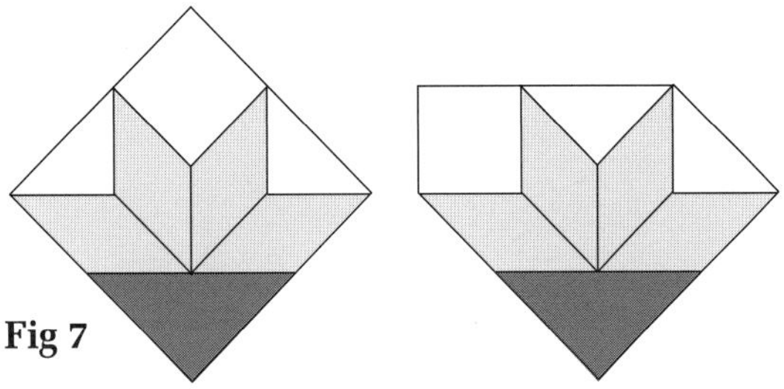

Fig 7

6. Sew a white Triangle (E) to two sides of the flower block with the Square (C) in middle, **Fig 8**.

7. Fold one 1 1/4" x 9 1/4" bias strip in half lengthwise with wrong sidestogether; press. Cut two 2 1/2" lengths from strip. Place raw edges of a shorter strip along upper edge one of the stem placement lines on a white Rectangle (F), **Fig 9**; stitch 1/4" from raw edge of strip,**Fig 10**.

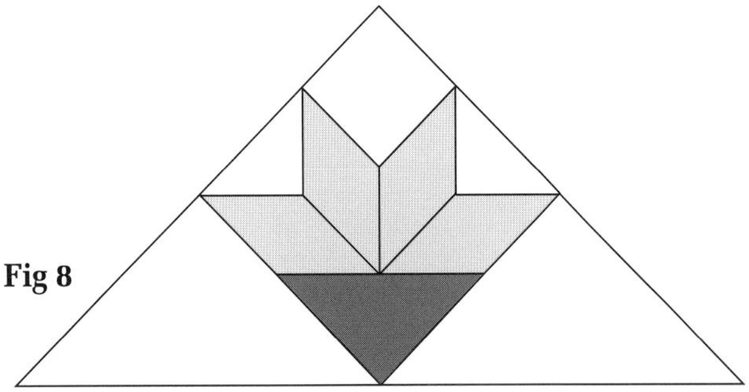

Fig 8

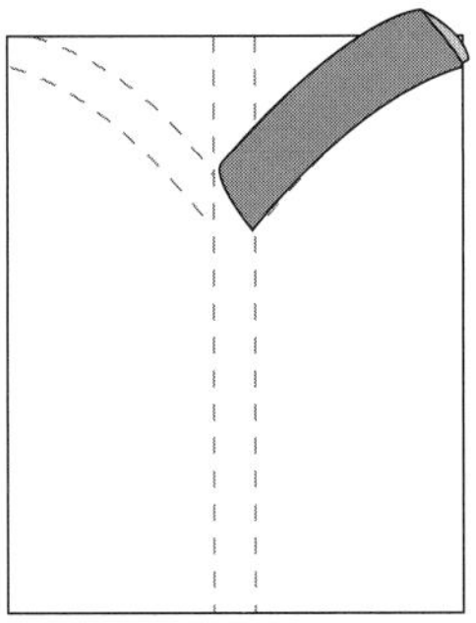

Fig 9

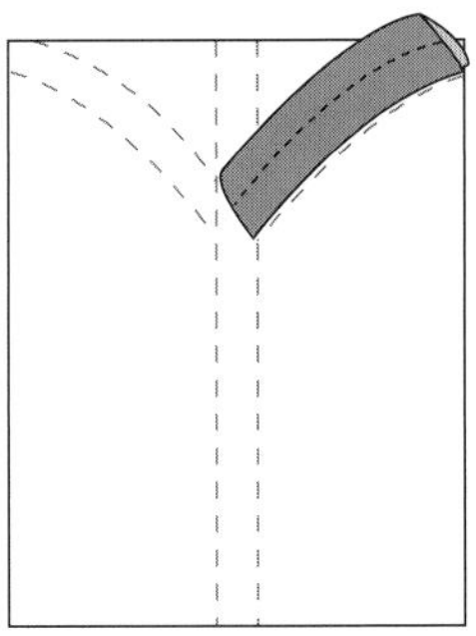

Fig 10

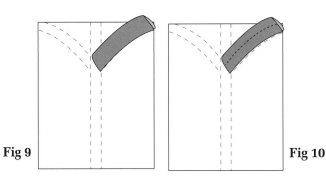

8. Fold strip over raw edges and appliqué (see Basic Appliqué, pages 5 and 6) in place, **Fig 11**.

9. Repeat for other short stem, then long stem; trim stems even with Rectangle, **Fig 12**.

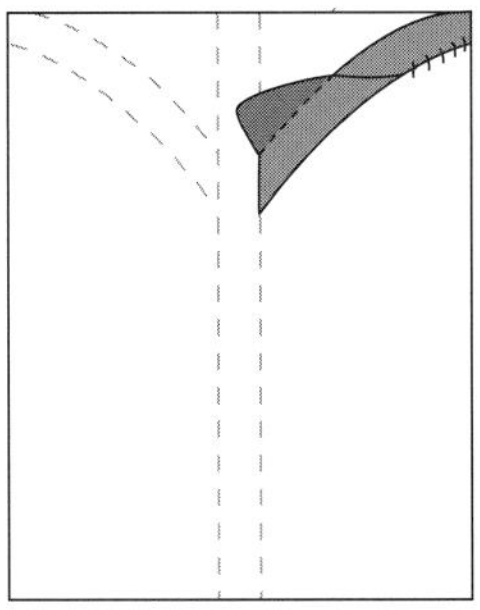

Fig 11

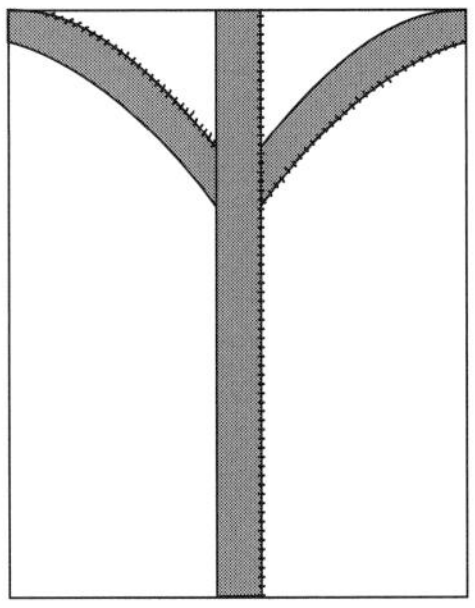

Fig 12

10. Sew a flower block on each long side of Rectangle (F), **Fig 13**. Note positions of Squares (C) in flower blocks.

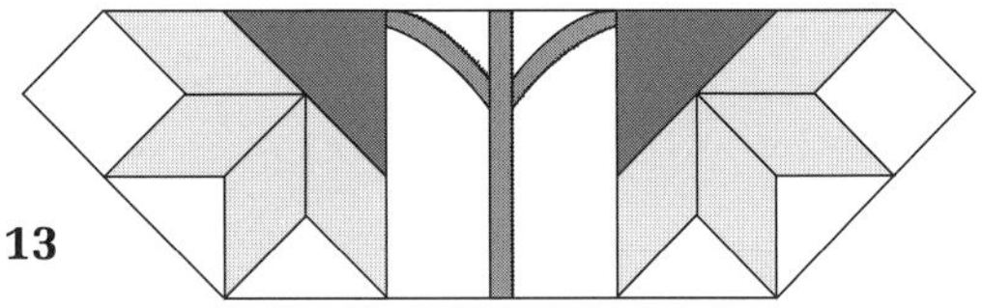

Fig 13

11. Sew flower block sections together, **Fig 14**.

Fig 14

12. Sew green Triangle (G) to lower edge, **Fig 15**.

Fig 15

13. Sew green Triangle (I) to short edge of white Rectangle (H); sew another green Triangle (I) to opposite short edge of another white Rectangle (H), **Fig 16**. Sew to adjacent edges of flower basket, **Fig 17**.

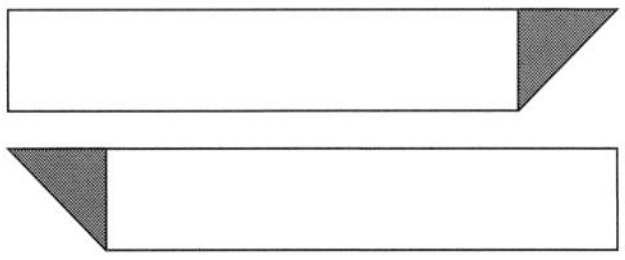

Fig 16

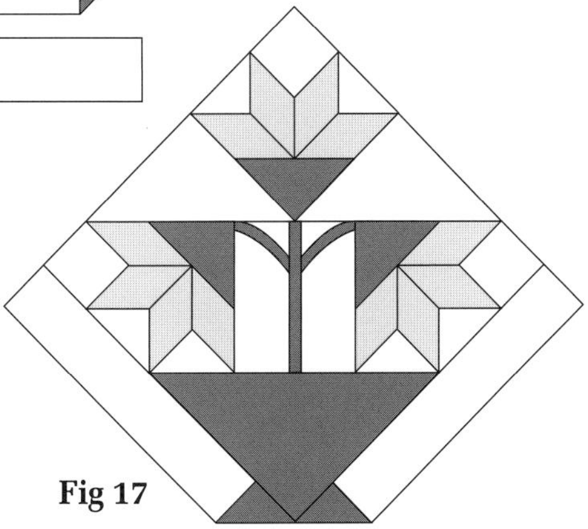

Fig 17

14. Sew white Triangle (J) to lower edge of block to complete Flower Basket, **Fig 18**.

15. Repeat steps 1 to 13 to complete four Flower Basket Blocks.

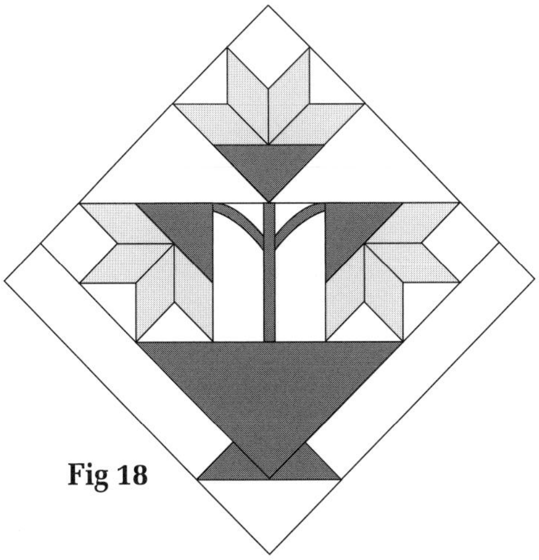

Fig 18

Border Basket Block

Make 32

1. Fold curved edges of Basket Handle (O) under 1/4"; finger press in place. Appliqué (see pages 6 and 7) onto a white Triangle (M), **Fig 19**. Sew to a pastel M Triangle, **Fig 20**.

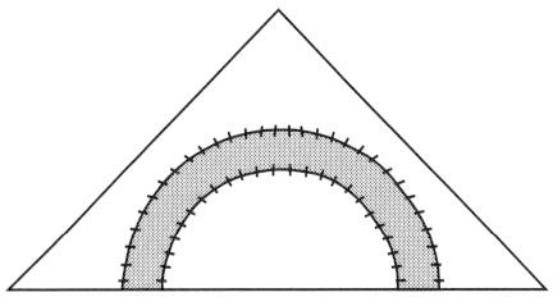

Fig 19

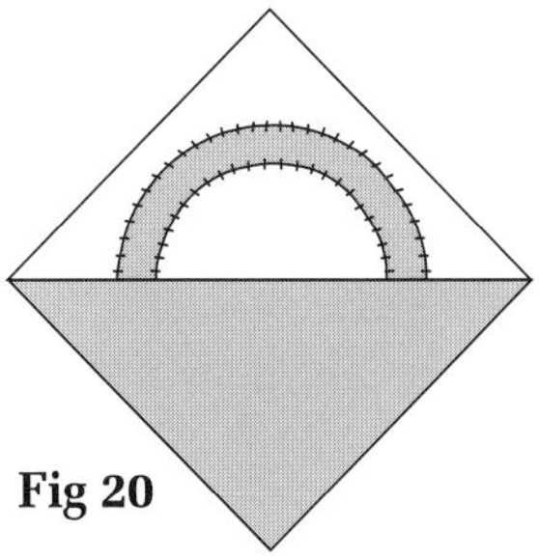

Fig 20

2. Sew a pastel Triangle (N) to short edge of a white Rectangle (K); sew another pastel Triangle (N) to opposite side of another white Rectangle (K), **Fig 21**. Sew to adjacent sides of pastel Triangle (M), **Fig 22**.

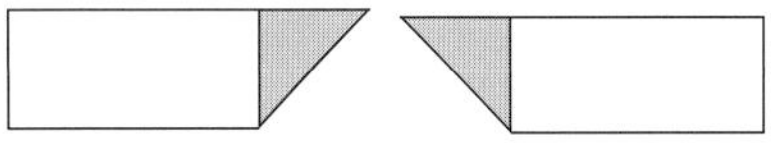

Fig 21

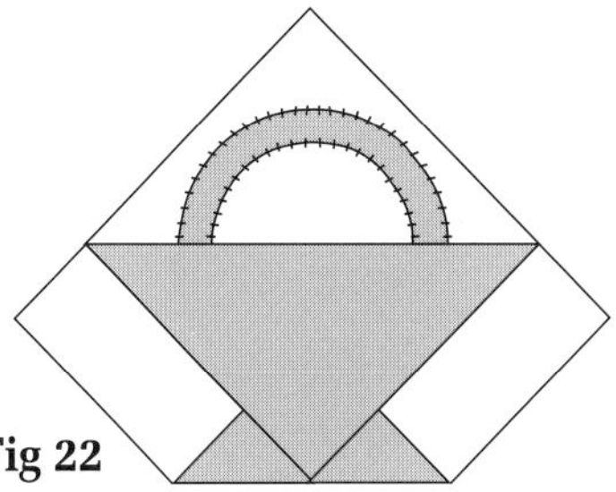

Fig 22

3. Sew white Triangle (L) to lower edge to complete Border Basket Block, **Fig 23**.

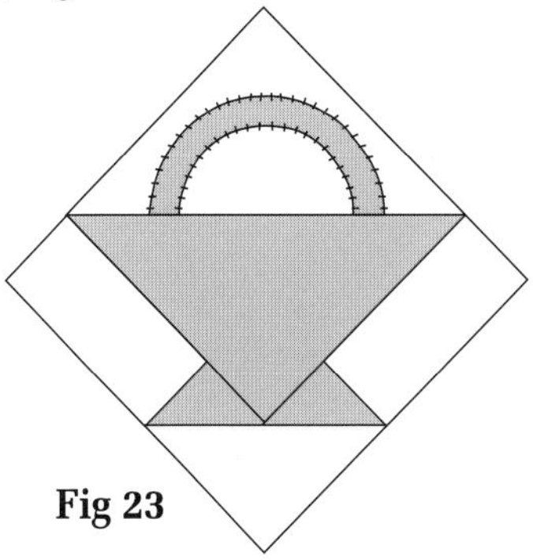

Fig 23

4. Repeat steps 1 to 3 to complete 32 Border Basket Blocks.

Yo-Yo Violets

Make 48

1. Fold raw edge of a purple Circle (Y) 1/8" toward wrong side; sew running stitch near fold, **Fig 24**.

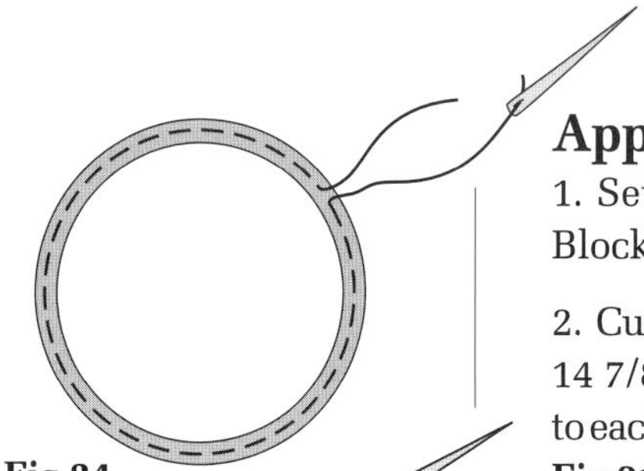

Fig 24

2. Pull thread to gather, **Fig 25**; knot thread, but do not cut.

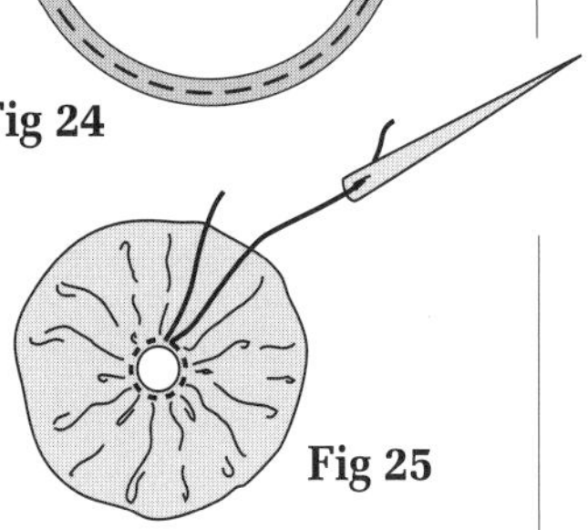

Fig 25

3. Wrap thread around outer edge toward back and bring thread up through center a couple times, pulling thread tightly, **Fig 26**. Repeat in three more places, **Fig 27**; knot thread.

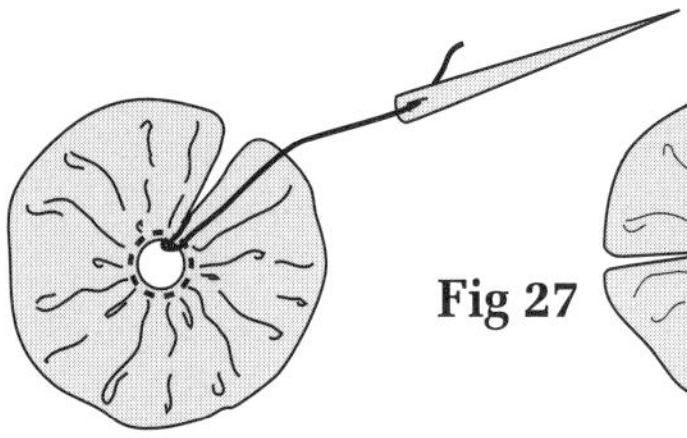

Fig 26

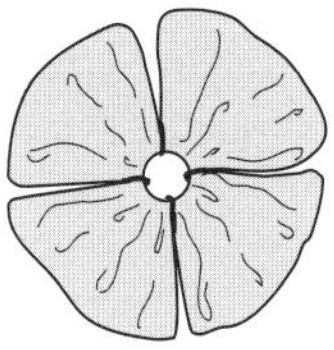

Fig 27

4. Repeat steps 1 to 3 for a total of 48 Violets.

Buds

Make sixteen

1. Fold a pink Z Square in half diagonally toward wrong side, **Fig 28**.

2. Bring two corners together to make a pleasing-looking bud; hand tack in place **Fig 29**.

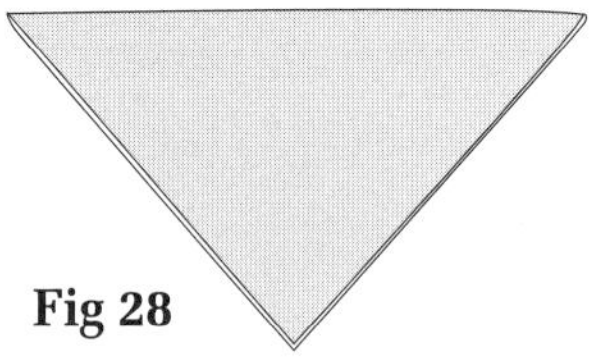

Fig 28

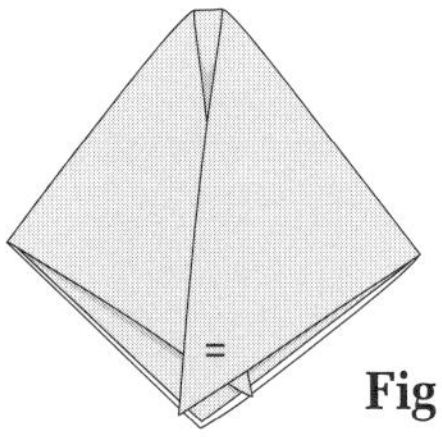

Fig 29

3. Repeat steps 1 and 2 for a total of sixteen Buds.

Appliquéing the Quilt

1. Sew the four Center Basket Blocks together.

2. Cut four white triangles with 14 7/8" legs, **Fig 30**; sew a triangle to each side of center Basket Blocks, **Fig 31**.

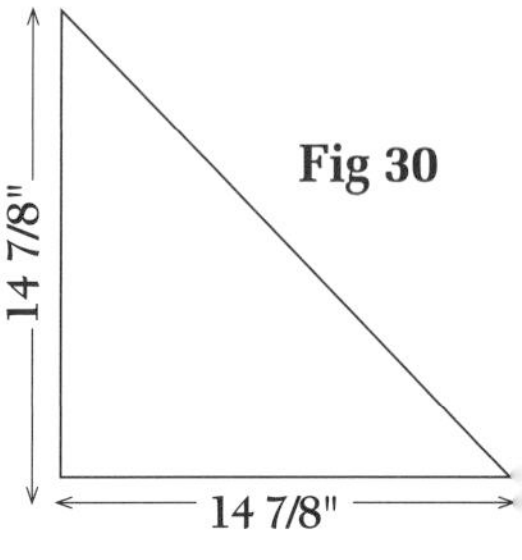
14 7/8"
14 7/8"

Fig 30

Fig 31

3. Referring to Placement Diagram, **Fig 32** (at bottom of this page), appliqué bias strips in place first. Appliqué Leaves next. Appliqué Buds at the top edge of stems, then appliqué Calyxes over lower edge of Buds.

4. Next, tack Yo-Yo Violets in clusters of three using matching thread and seed beads, **Fig 33**. Bring thread up from back through center of violet; place bead on needle and go back through violet center. Repeat twice for a total of three beads in center of each violet.

5. Appliqué Bow last.

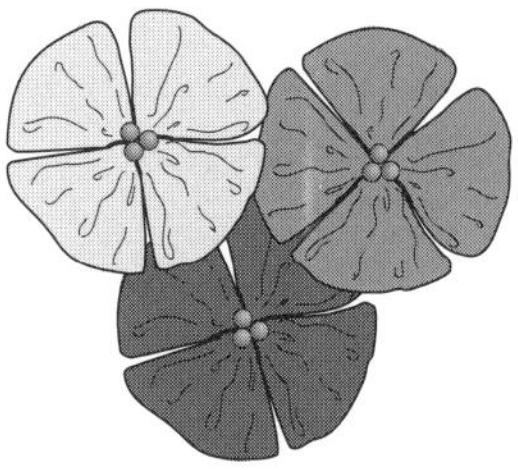

Fig 33

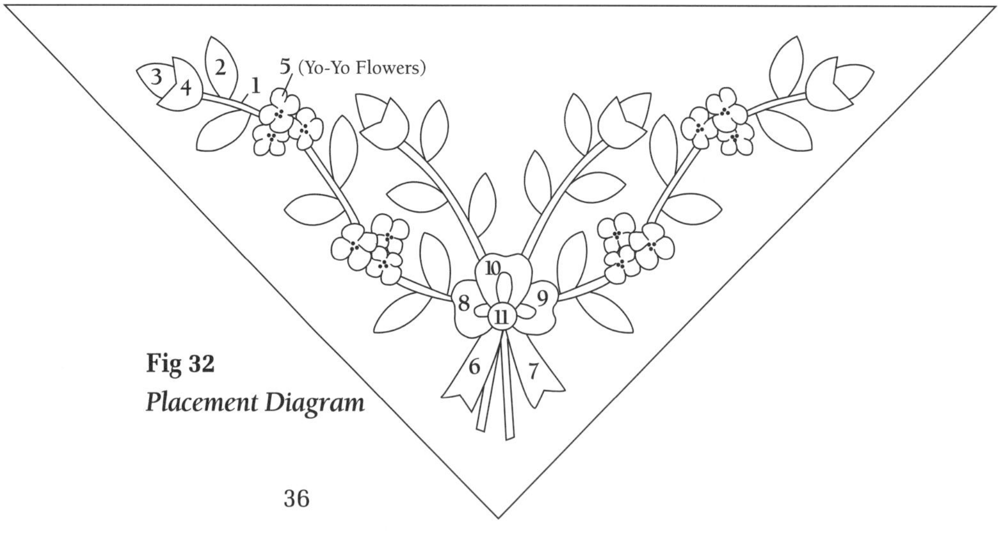
3
4
2
1
5 (Yo-Yo Flowers)
10
8
11
9
6
7

Fig 32
Placement Diagram

Adding Borders

1. Referring to Layout, sew pink border strips to sides first, then to top and bottom.

2. For Basket Border, sew seven Basket Blocks, twelve Border Triangles (P), and two Corner Triangles together for each side, **Fig 34**. Sew to sides of quilt.

3. Sew fourteen white Border Triangles (P) to seven Basket blocks for top and bottom borders, **Fig 35**. Sew to top and bottom.

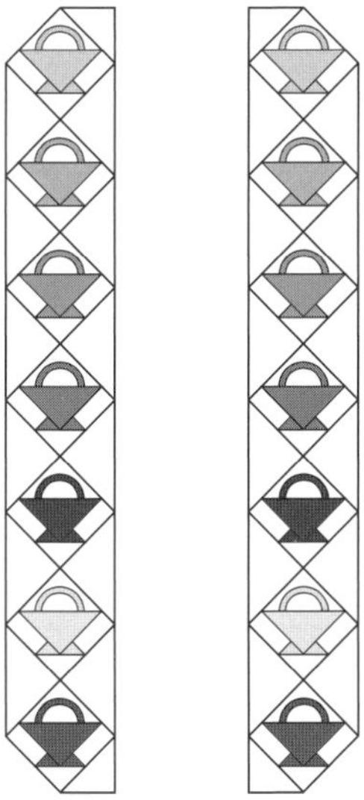
Left Border Right Border

Fig 34

Top Border

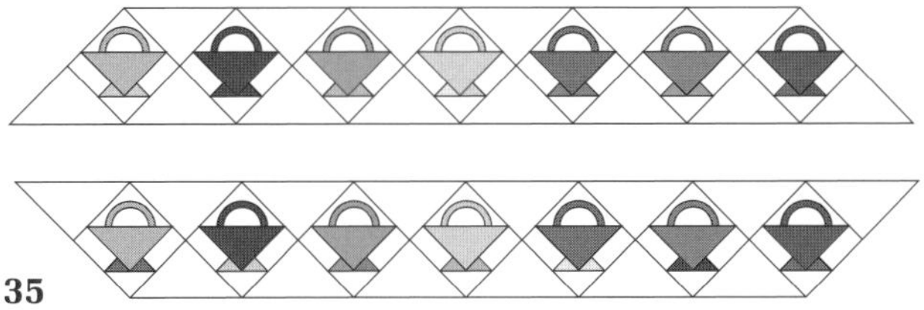

Fig 35

Bottom Border

4. For each corner, sew a white Border Triangle to opposite sides of a Border Basket Block; then sew a corner triangle to adjacent side, **Fig 36**. Sew to each corner.

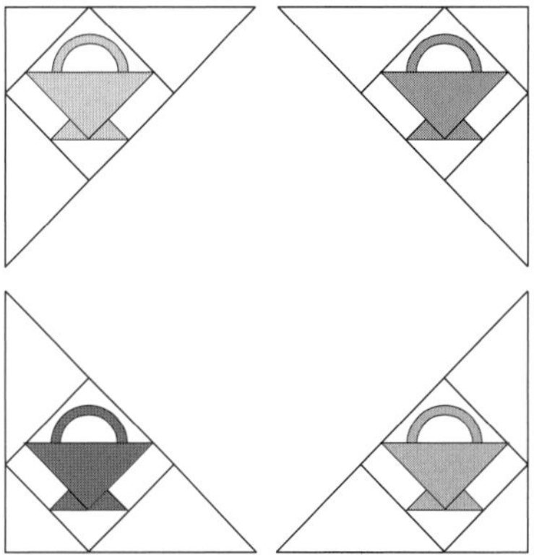

Fig 36

Finishing the Quilt

See General Directions starting with Preparing the Quilt Top, page 6, to finish quilt.Photographed quilt was quilted with diagonal cross hatching in central portion of quilt. The Fleur de Lis Quilting Pattern on page 38, was used in the Border Triangles (Q).

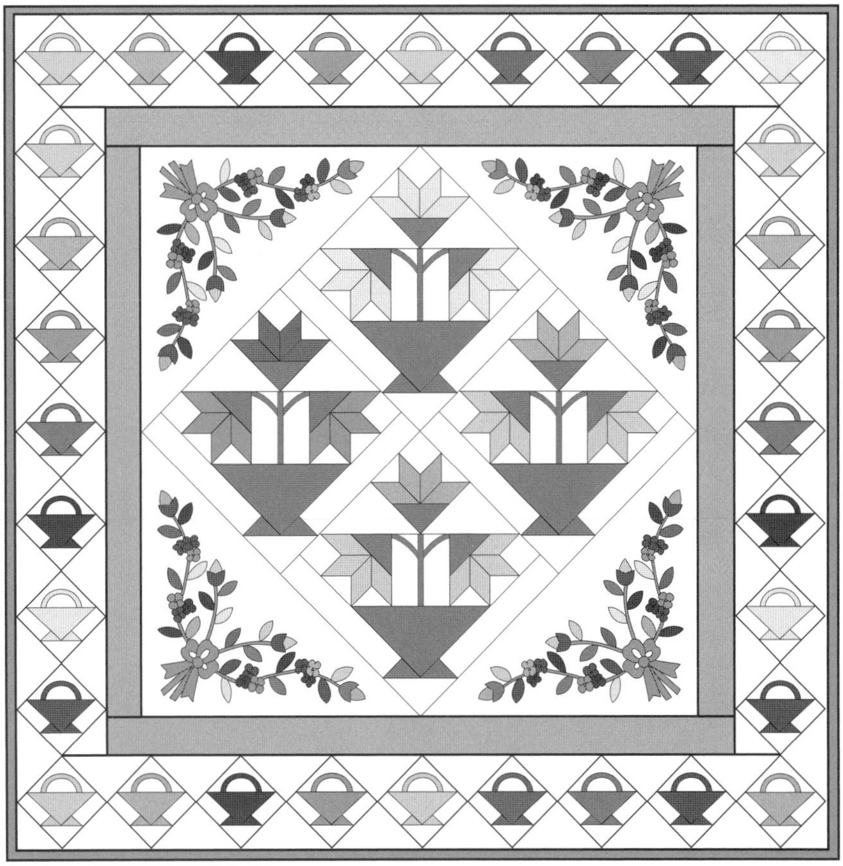

Quilt Layout

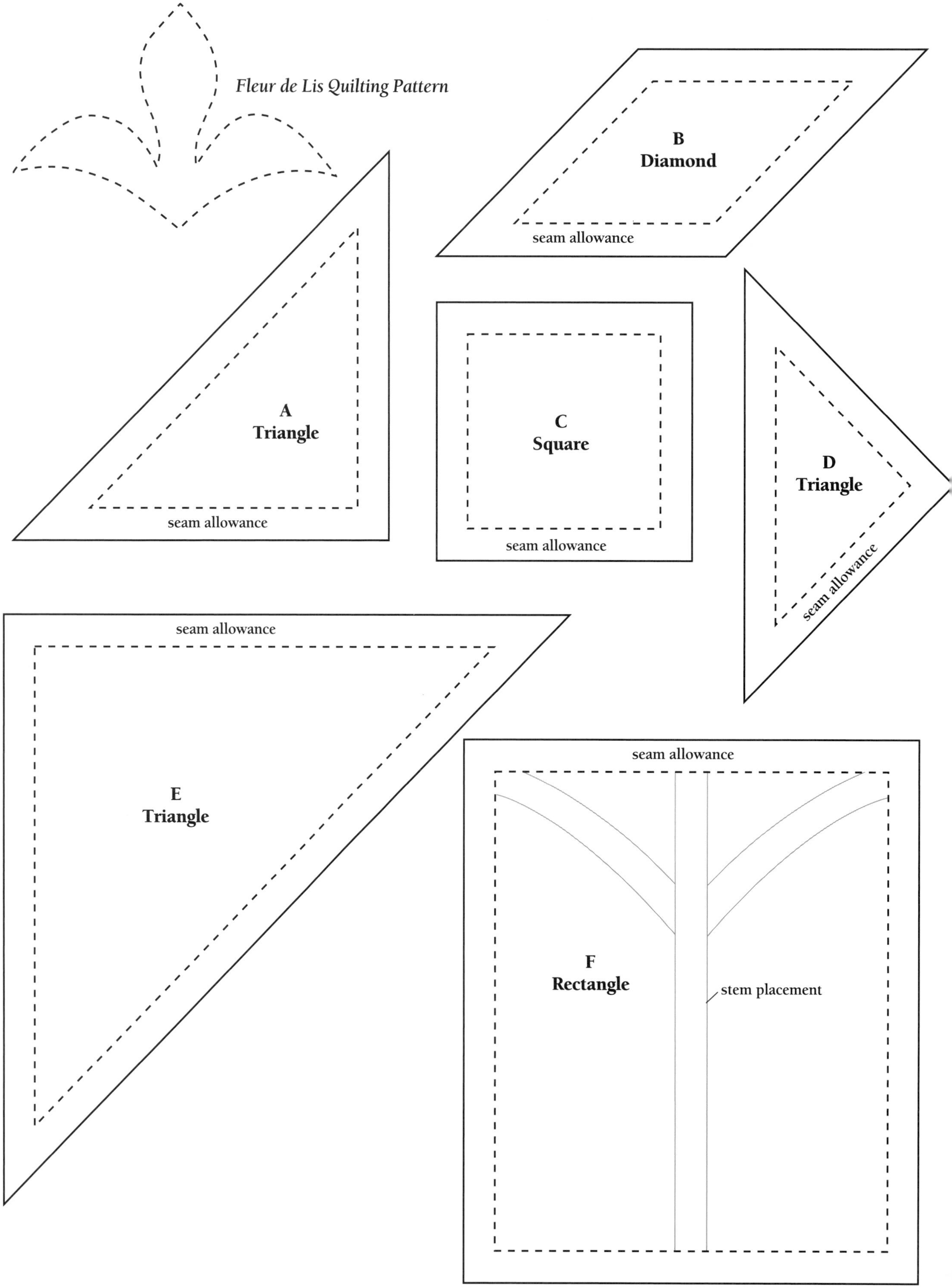

Fleur de Lis Quilting Pattern
B
Diamond
seam allowance
A
Triangle
seam allowance
C
Square
seam allowance
D
Triangle
seam allowance
seam allowance
E
Triangle
seam allowance
F
Rectangle
stem placement

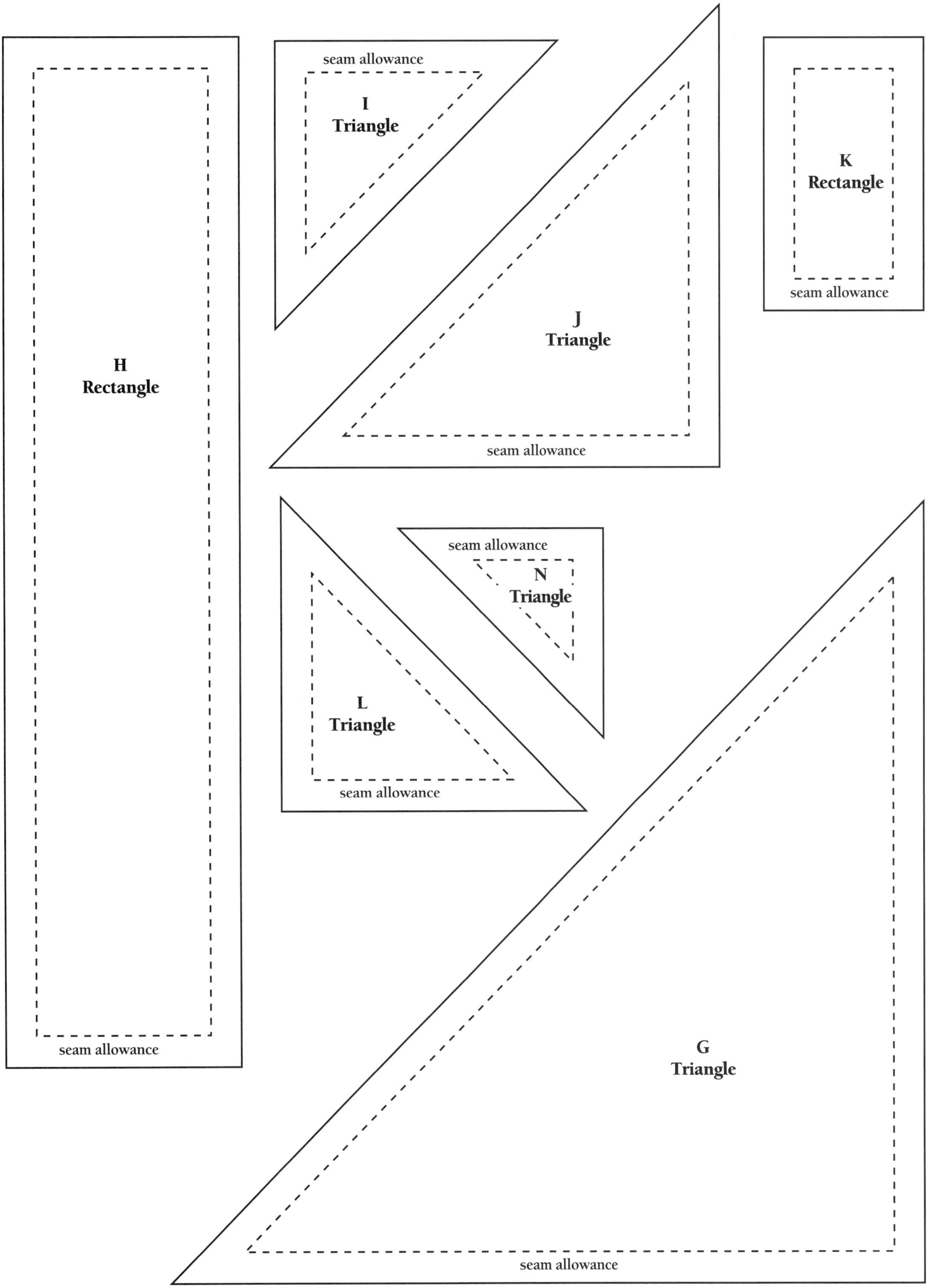
H
Rectangle
seam allowance
seam allowance
I
Triangle
J
Triangle
seam allowance
K
Rectangle
seam allowance
seam allowance
N
Triangle
L
Triangle
seam allowance
G
Triangle
seam allowance

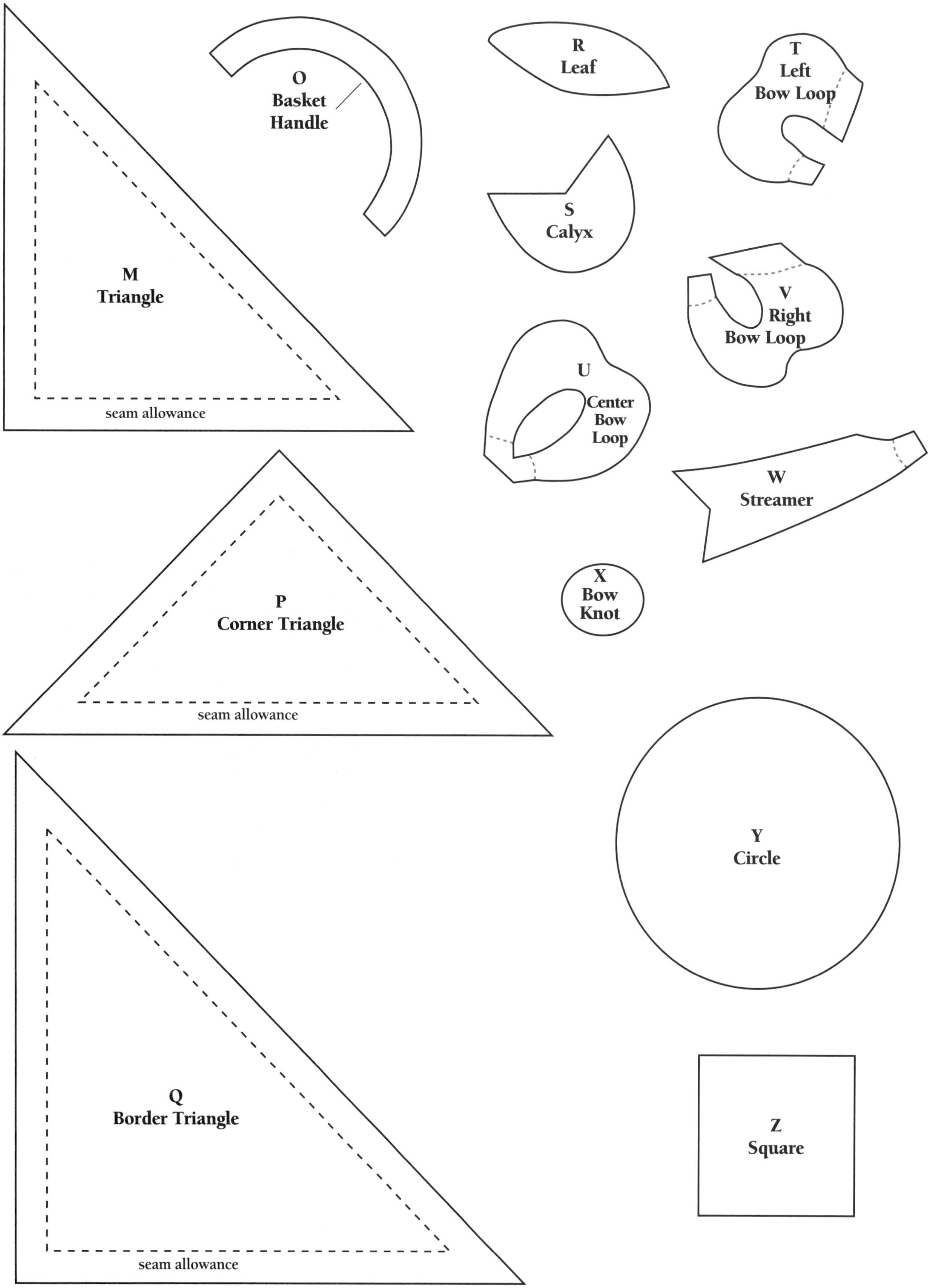
M
Triangle
seam allowance
O
Basket
Handle
R
Leaf
T
Left
Bow Loop
S
Calyx
V
Right
Bow Loop
U
Center
Bow
Loop
W
Streamer
P
Corner Triangle
seam allowance
X
Bow
Knot
Y
Circle
Q
Border Triangle
seam allowance
Z
Square

Jeannie's Summer Basket

Baltimore Basket

Heirloom Basket

Des Paniers Bleus

Shown in color on page 42

Baltimore Basket

by Sheri Wilkinson Lalk
Honorable Mention
Approximate Size: 40" x 40"

"I've always loved the Baltimore Album Quilts. When I found out the theme for the contest was baskets, a Baltimore Basket *was the first thing that came to mind. Hearts and flowers are something that I love to use in everything I make."*

Fabric Requirements:

3 yds muslin or light print (background and backing)
1 yd med blue print (basket, binding and flowers)
1/3 yd dk rust print (hearts and flowers)
1/4 yd mauve solid (flowers, bows and buds)
scraps lt peach print, black print, tan print and rust solid (flowers, heart and flower centers)
1/4 yd lt blue pin dot (tulips, bird)
1/4 yd pale blue solid (tulips, bird)
1/2 yd lt green solid (stems, leaves)
1/3 yd med green solid (stems, leaves)
1/4 yd med green print (leaves)
1/4 yd dk green print (leaves, calyxes)

Additional Supplies:

dk blue embroidery floss (bird's eye)
med green embroidery floss (small stems)

Pattern Pieces (pages 48 to 52):

A Large Heart
B Small Heart
C Large Flower
D Large Flower Calyx
E Outer Flower
F Middle Flower

G Flower Center
H Small Flower
I Small Flower Center
J Bud
K Bud Calyx
L Medium Flower
M Medium Flower Calyx
N Outer Tulip
O Tulip Center
P Bird Body
Q Upper Wing
R Lower Wing
S Middle Bow Loop
T Side Bow Loops
U Bow Streamers
V Bow Knot
W Wavy Leaf
X Medium Leaf
Y Medium Leaf with Curve
Z Large Leaf
AA Small Leaf
BB Tiny Leaf
CC (1,2) Basket Rim
DD Basket Base
EE (1, 2) Basket Placement

Cutting Requirements:

one 42" square, background fabric
one Large Heart (A), dk rust
seven Small Hearts (B), dk rust
one Small Heart (B), black print
three Large Flowers (C), dk rust
three Large Flower Calyxes (D), dk green
eight Outer Flower (E), mauve
eight Middle Flower (F), black print
eight Center Flower (G), lt peach print
nine Small Flowers (H), tan print
nine Small Flower Centers (I), rust print
five Buds (J), mauve
five Bud Calyxes (K), med green solid
twelve Medium Flowers (L), med blue print
twelve Medium Flower Calyxes (M), med green print
five Outer Tulips (N), lt blue pin dot
five Tulip Centers (O), pale blue solid
one Bird Body (P), lt blue pin dot
one Upper Wing (Q), pale blue solid
one Lower Wing (R), pale blue solid
one Middle Bow Loop (S), mauve
two Side Bow Loops (T), mauve
two Bow Streamers (U), mauve
two Bow Knots (V), mauve
four Wavy Leaves (W), med green print
41 Medium Leaves (X), med green print
eight Medium Leaves with Curve (Y), dk green print
six Large Leaves (Z), lt green solid
eight Large Leaves (Z), med green solid
34 Small Leaves (AA), med green print
six Tiny Leaves (BB), lt green solid
one Basket Rim (CC), med blue print
one Basket Base (DD), med blue print
1/2"-wide bias strips, med blue print
1/2"-wide bias strips, med green solid
1/2"-wide bias strips, med green print

Instructions

Appliquéing the Quilt

***Note:** Read Basic Appliqué, pages 5 and 6, before beginning to appliqué.*

1. Fold 42" background square in half, then in half again, **Fig 1**. Finger press folds to make creases. This will aid in placing appliqué design.

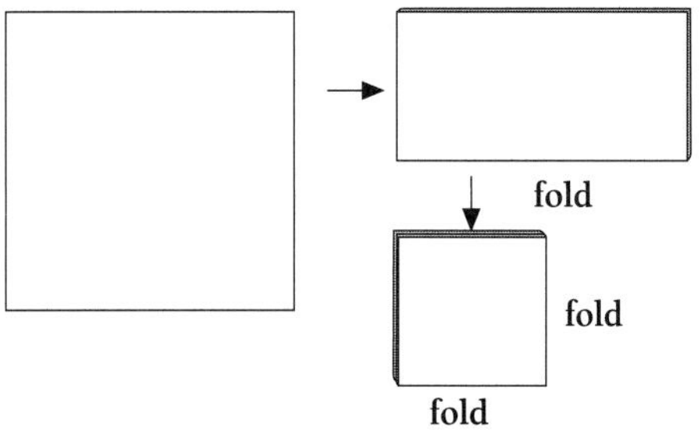
fold
fold
fold

Fig 1

2. Using pattern pieces CC, DD and EE, draw basket on right side of background square, **Fig 2**. Draw remaining flowers, leaves, stems, hearts, bows and bird, referring to **Fig 3** on the next page.

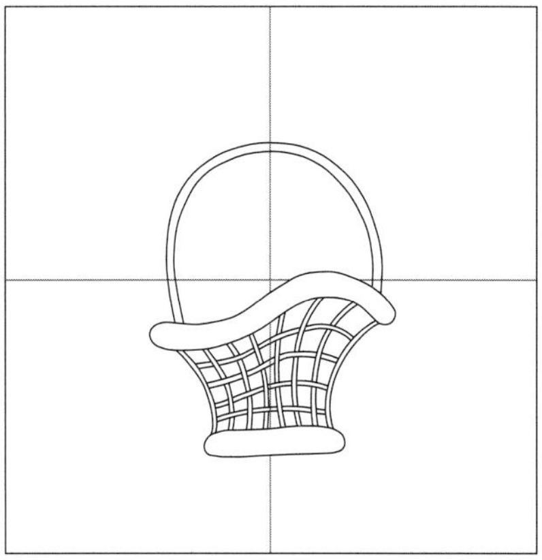

Fig 2

3. Appliqué basket first. Fold both long edges of med blue print bias strips under 1/8". Place folded strips along drawn lines, weaving strips in and out for a basket effect (refer to Basket Placement pattern EE which has dotted lines that represent areas that are overlapped by another piece); pin strips in place. Appliqué along all folded edges. Appliqué Basket Rim and Basket Base in place.

4. Appliqué flowers, leaves, stems, and basket bow in order: med green bias strips; Wavy Leaves (W); Small Leaves (AA); Medium Leaves with Curve (Y); Large Leaves (Z); Buds (J); Bud Calyxes (K); Outer Tulips (N); Tulip Centers (D); Large

Flower (C); Large Flower Calyx (D); Outer Flowers (E); Middle Flowers (F); Flower Centers (G); Small Flowers (H); Small Flower Centers (I); Tiny Leaves (BB); Middle Bow Loop (S); Side Bow Loops (T); Bow Streamers (U); and Bow Knot (V).

5. Appliqué Upper Wing (Q), Bird Body (P), and Lower Wing (R).

6. Appliqué med green bias strips around basket; then appliqué Medium Flowers (L); Medium Flower Calyxes (M); Large Heart (A); Small Hearts (B); Side Bow Loops (T); Bow Streamers (U); Bow Knot (V) and Medium Leaves (X).

7. Referring to dashed lines on Placement Diagram below, embroider stems for Small Flowers with Chain Stitch using six strands of med green embroidery floss, **Fig 4**.

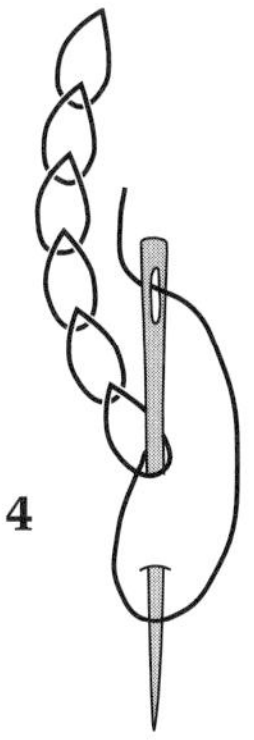

Fig 4

X
X
B
B
L
M
S
T
V
I
H
Q
P
R
U
AA
J
K
W
C
D
N
O
E
F
G
Z
Y
Y
CC
BB
DD
A
B
T
V
U

Fig 3

Basket Placement Diagram

Finishing the Quilt

Refer to General Directions starting with preparing the Quilt Top, page 6 to finish quilt. Photographed quilt was quilted diagonally in both directions.

Quilt Layout

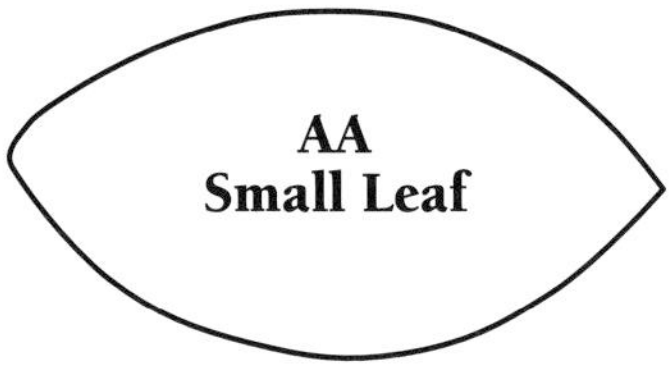
AA
Small Leaf

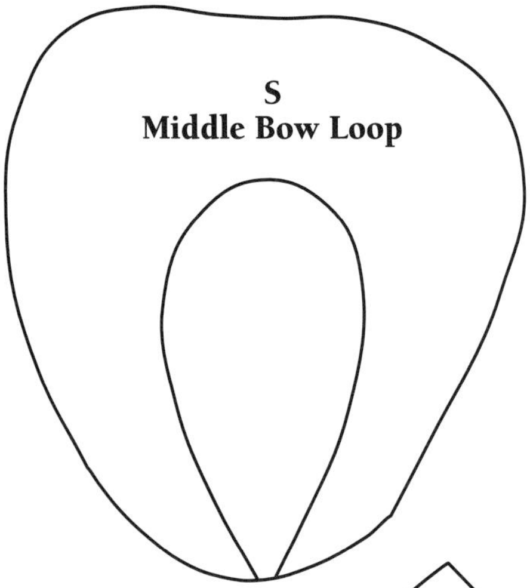
S
Middle Bow Loop

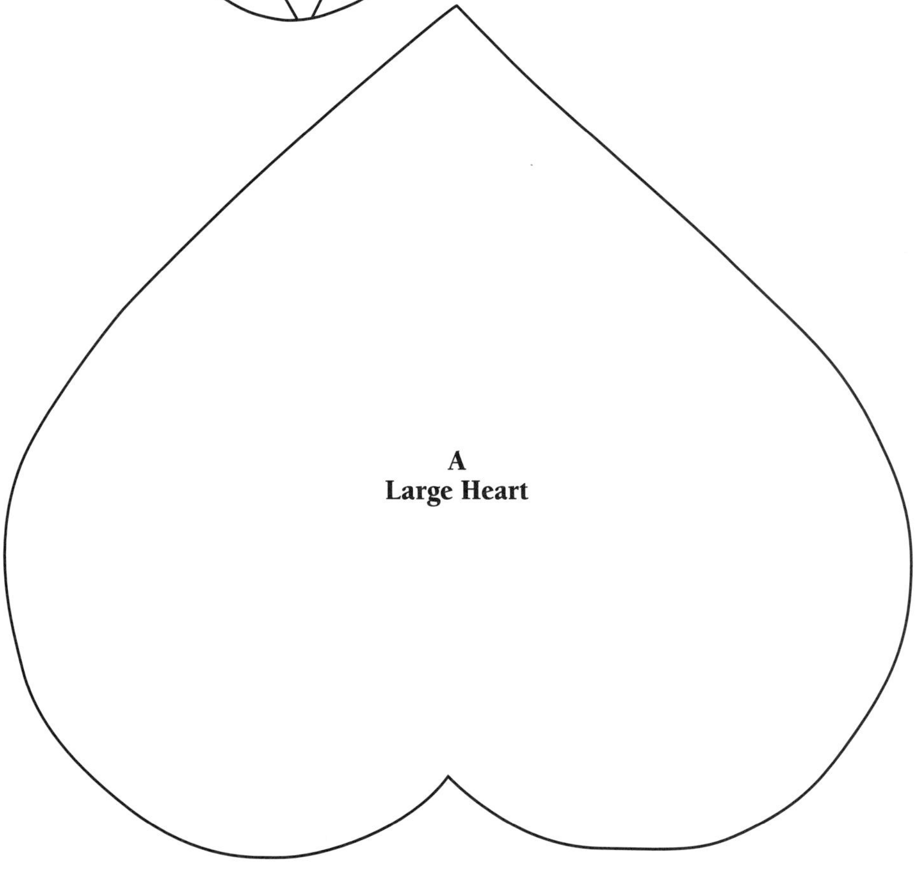
A
Large Heart

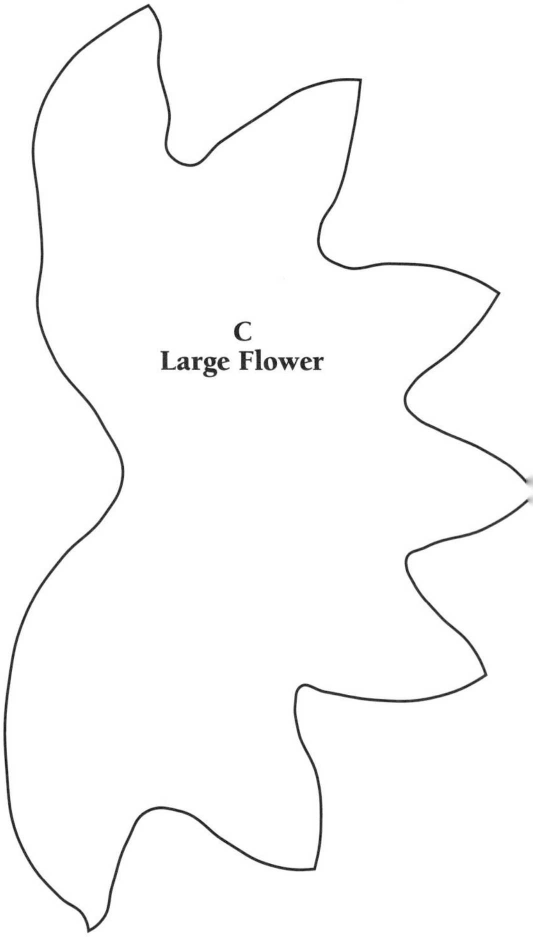
C
Large Flower

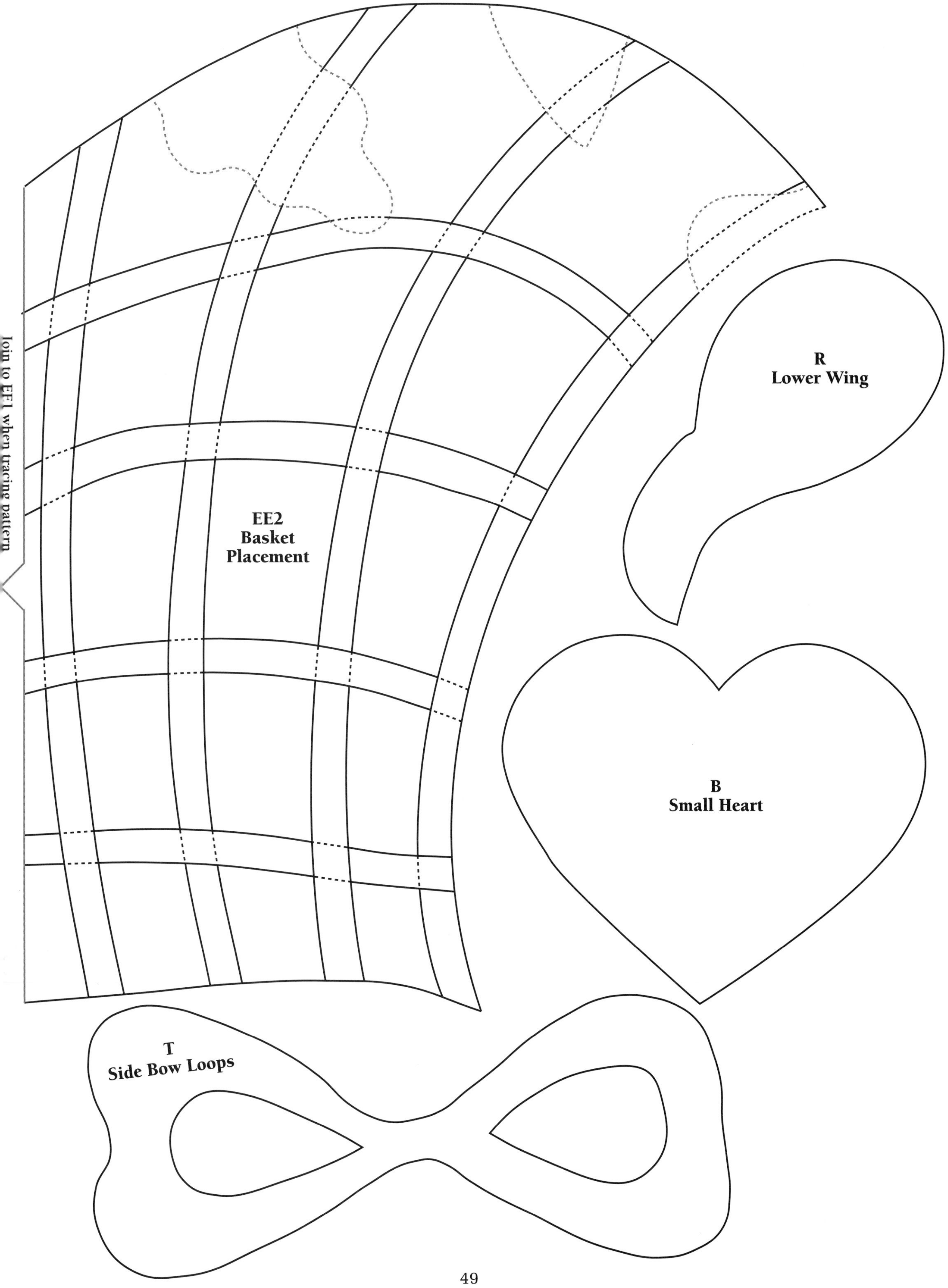
Join to EF1 when tracing pattern
R
Lower Wing
EE2
Basket
Placement
B
Small Heart
T
Side Bow Loops

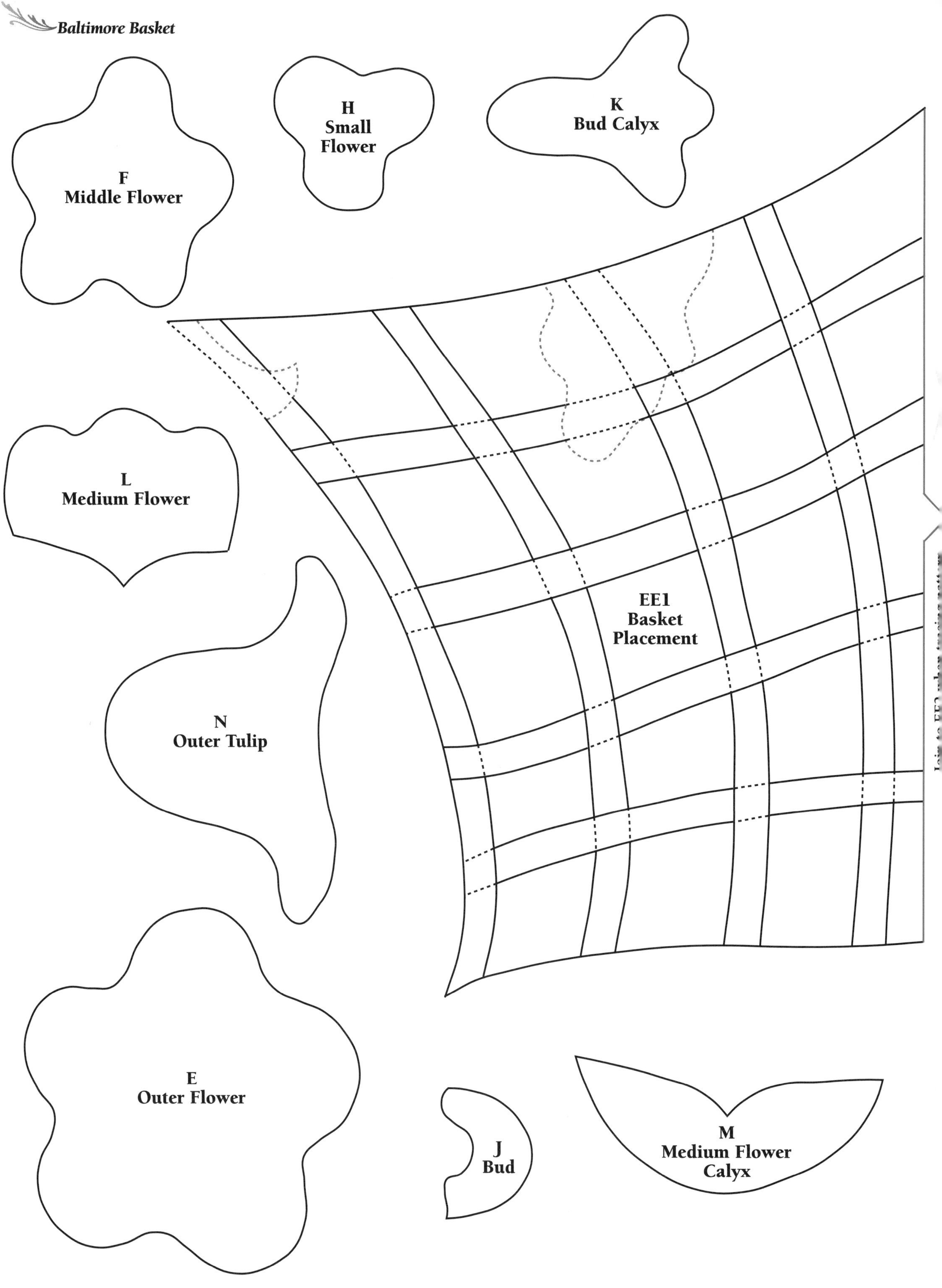

F
Middle Flower
H
Small
Flower
K
Bud Calyx
L
Medium Flower
EE1
Basket
Placement
N
Outer Tulip
E
Outer Flower
J
Bud
M
Medium Flower
Calyx

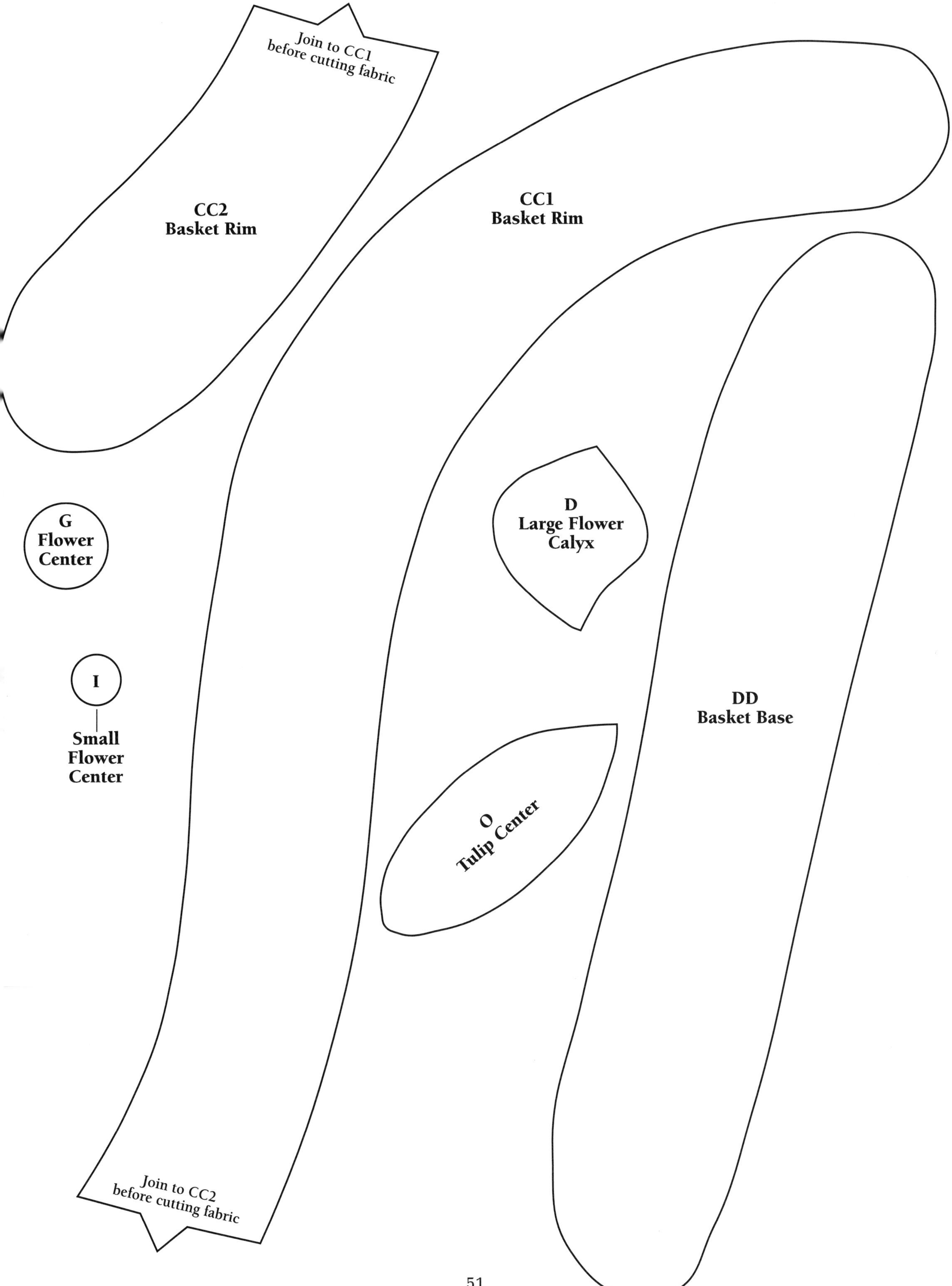
Join to CC1 before cutting fabric
CC2 Basket Rim
CC1 Basket Rim
G Flower Center
I
Small Flower Center
D Large Flower Calyx
DD Basket Base
O Tulip Center
Join to CC2 before cutting fabric

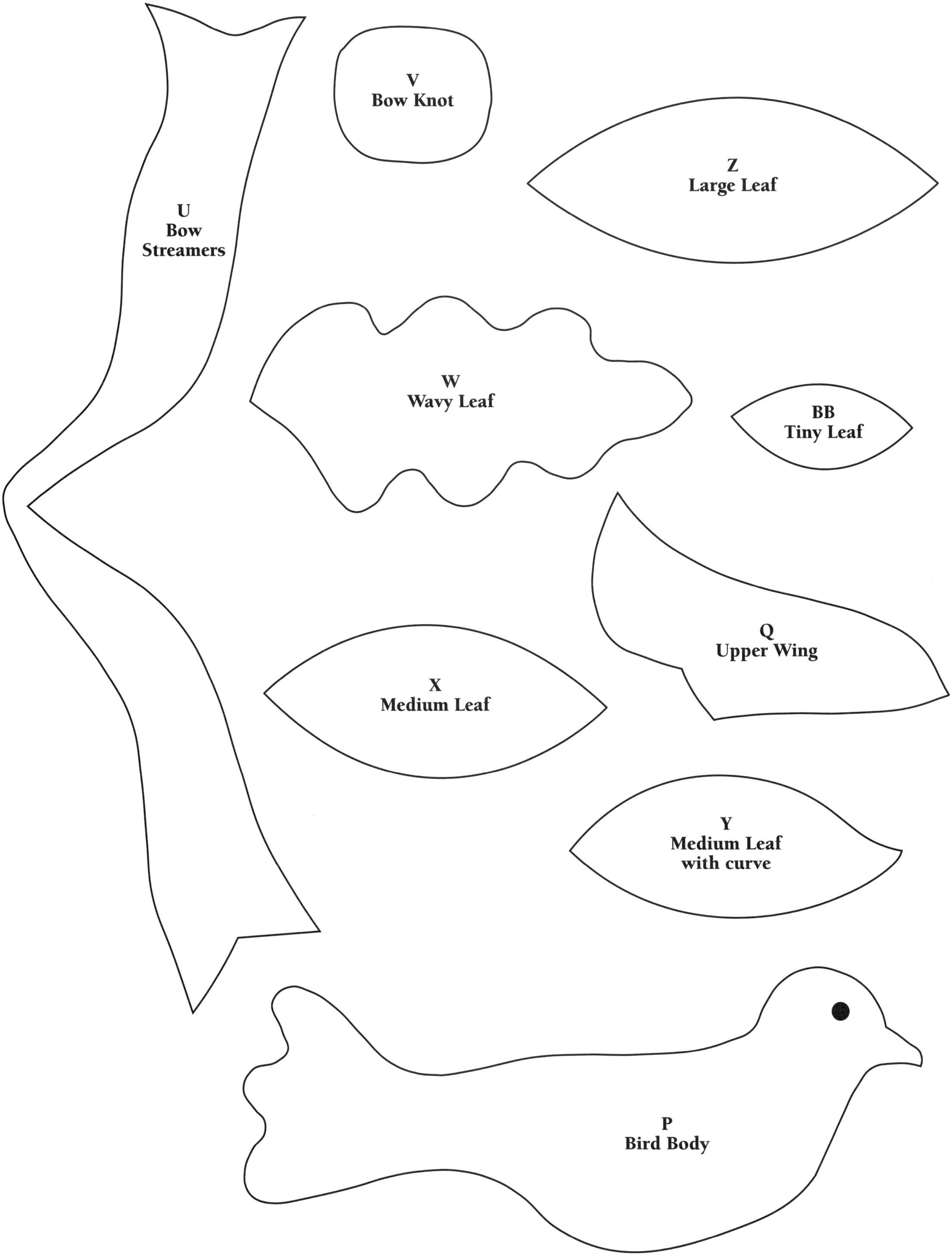
U
Bow
Streamers
V
Bow Knot
Z
Large Leaf
W
Wavy Leaf
BB
Tiny Leaf
Q
Upper Wing
X
Medium Leaf
Y
Medium Leaf
with curve
P
Bird Body

This quilt was based on a quilt by Kandy Peterson that appeared in Quilts! Quilts!! Quilts!!! *by Diana McClun and Laura Nownes; published by The Quilt Digest Press, 1988 who gave us special permission to use this design.*

Shown in color on page 44

Des Paniers Bleus

by Julia Cousins
Finalist
Approximate Size: 46" x 58"

"Des Paniers Bleus *(Blue Baskets - it sounds pretty in French) is the first quilt I've ever entered in a contest and I'm thrilled to be a finalist! I used the Postage Stamp Baskets block pattern with 48 different blue calicoes on a bleached muslin background. The blocks were machine pieced, with hand-appliquéd handles. I am pleased to say that this is the quilt upon which I finally mastered making my quilting stitches using that 'rocking' motion I kept hearing about. I played with all of my blue colors and values in order to give the impression that the baskets faded into the background at the edges."*

Fabric Requirements:

7 1/2 yds muslin (background, border, backing and binding)
1 1/2 yds basket fabric (or scraps to total 1 1/2 yds)

Cutting Requirements:

48 - 4 7/8" squares, basket fabric; cut in half diagonally (for large basket triangles)
48 - 2 7/8" squares, basket fabric; cut in half diagonally (for small basket triangles)
96 - 2 1/2" squares, muslin
48 - 4 7/8" squares, muslin; cut in half diagonally (for large basket triangles)
five 6"- wide strips, muslin (border)
six 3 1/2" - wide crosswise strips, muslin (binding)

Instructions

Basket

***Note:** Use the same fabric within each basket.*

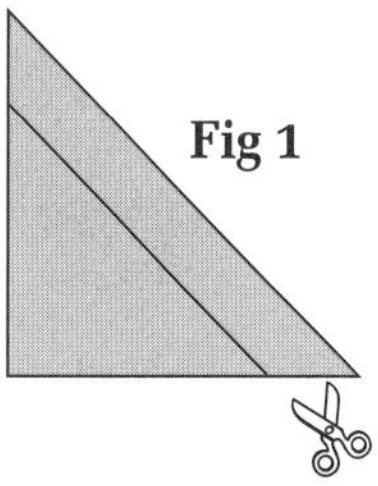

Fig 1

1. For handles, cut a 1 1/2"-wide bias strip from each of 48 large basket fabric triangles, **Fig 1**. Save remaining triangles for another project.

2. Fold bias strip in half lengthwise with wrong sides together. Stitch along length of strip, creating a tube, **Fig 2**.

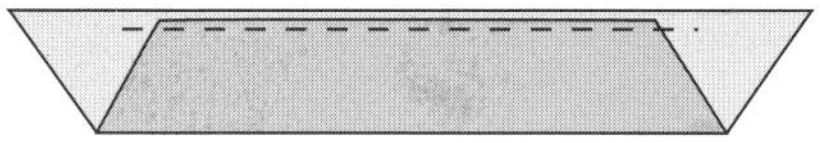

Fig 2

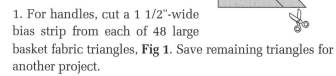

3. Center the seam on back of the tube and press flat, **Fig 3**.

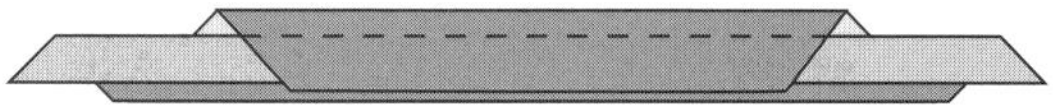

Fig 3

4. Center handle on muslin triangle, using steam iron to press tube into a curve, **Fig 4**.

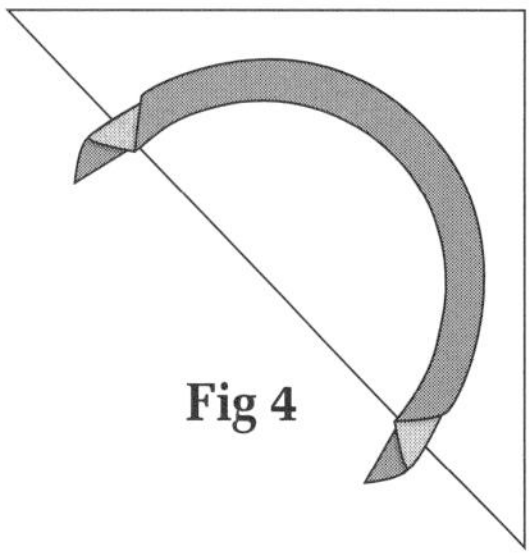

Fig 4

5. Appliqué handle onto triangle referring to Basic Appliqué, pages 6 and 7.

6. Sew large muslin and large basket triangle together, creating a square for main basket portion, **Fig 5**. Press seam toward darker fabric.

7. Sew small basket triangle to left side of muslin square; sew small basket triangle to right side of muslin square, **Fig 6**.

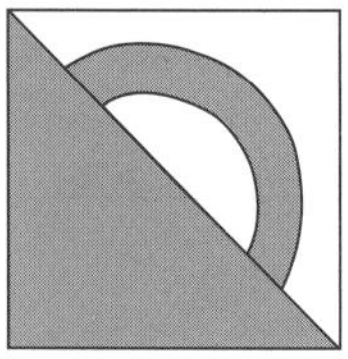

Fig 5

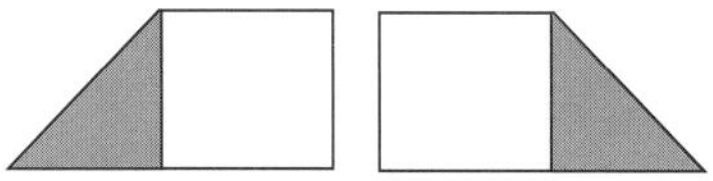

Fig 6

8. Stitch units made in step 7 to adjacent sides of main basket portion, **Fig 7**.

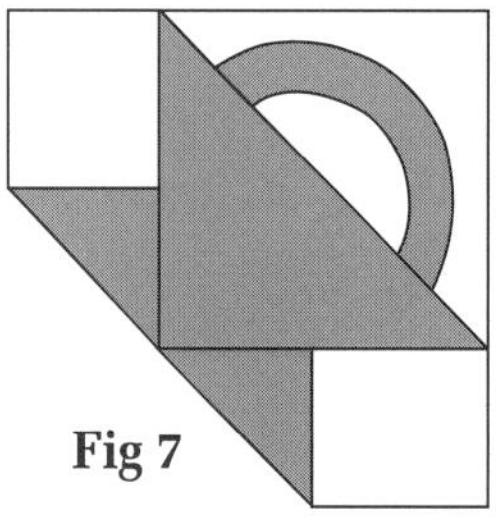

Fig 7

9. Stitch bias edge of a muslin triangle to base of basket, creating a 6 1/2" square Basket Block, **Fig 8**.

10. Repeat steps 2 to 9 for a total of 48 Basket Blocks.

11. Sew four Basket Blocks with handles facing inward to create Postage Stamp Block, **Fig 9**.

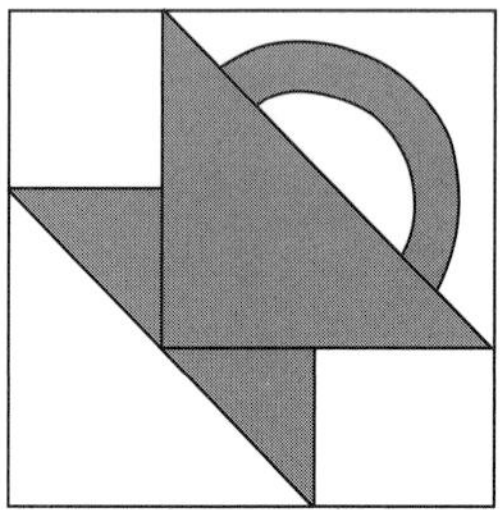

Fig 8 Basket Block

12. Repeat step 11 for a total of twelve Postage Stamp Blocks.

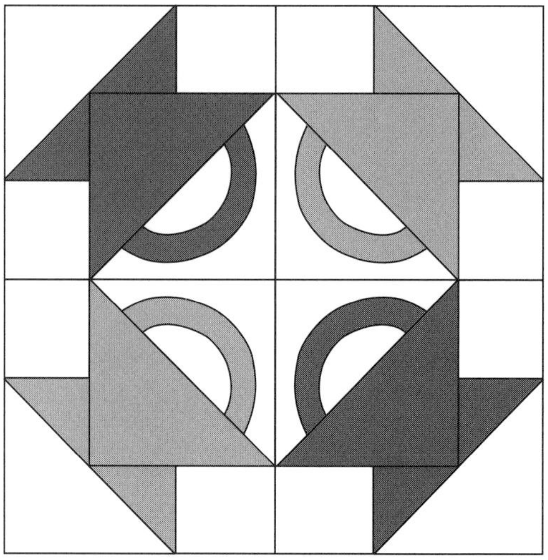

Fig 9 Postage Stamp Block

Finishing

1. Referring to Layout on next page, sew blocks together in rows of three blocks; sew rows together.

2. For mitered corners, place 6"-wide border strip along side of quilt, placing strip 6" beyond sides of quilt, **Fig 10**; begin and end stitching 1/4" from quilt top, **Fig 11**. Repeat for remaining side of quilt.

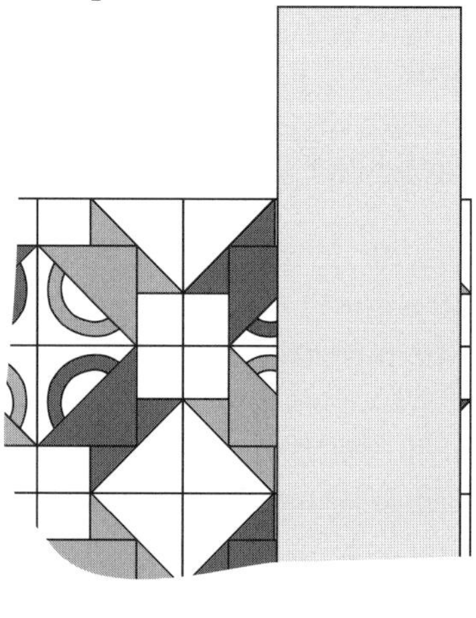

Fig 10

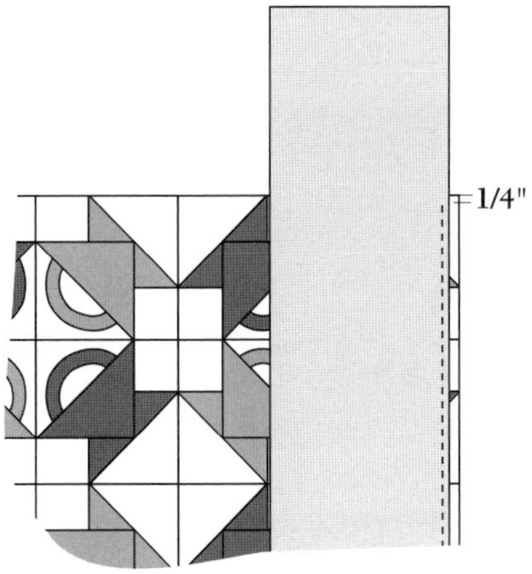
1/4"

Fig 11

3. Miter corners, sewing from inner corner toward outer edge, **Fig 12**; trim excess fabric.

4. Refer to General Directions starting with Preparing the Quilt Top, page 6, to complete your quilt.

Fig 12

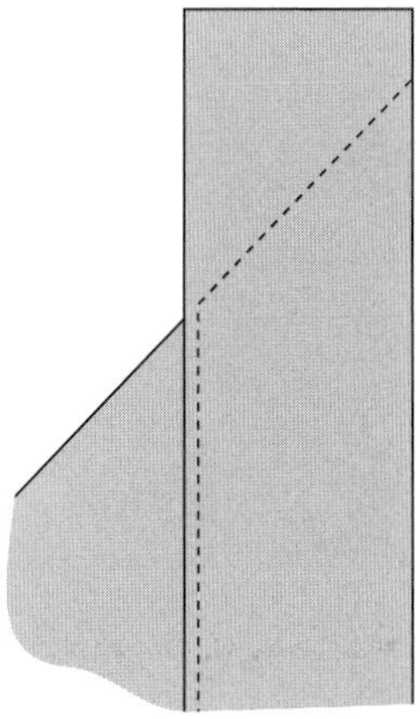

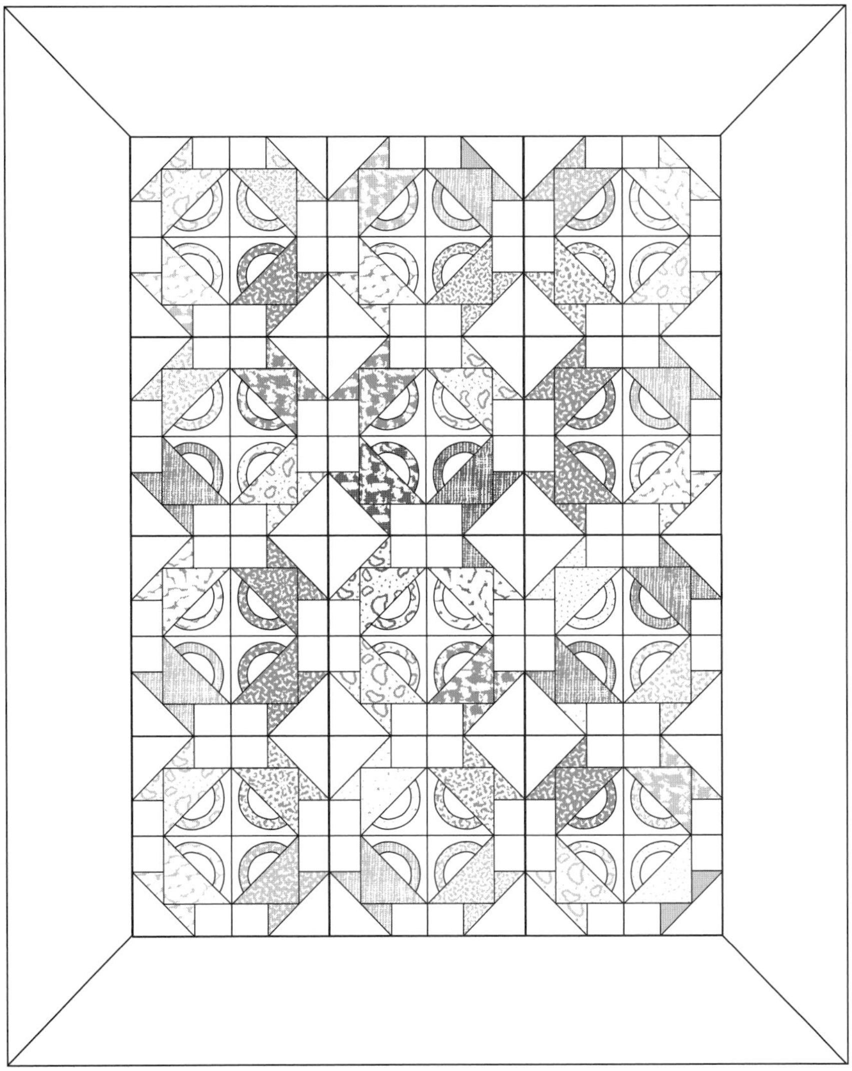

Quilt Layout

Heirloom Basket

by Ruth Diane Hosfield
Finalist
Approximate Size: 41" x 47"

"The original double bed quilt pattern by Ann Orr was featured in Good Housekeeping magazine in January, 1935. When I saw a picture of it, I just had to make a wall hanging. I designed my pattern on graph paper using a magnifying glass to see the various shades necessary to make a beautiful flower basket. The style is called cross stitch. My quilt consists of 2,322 - 1 1/8" squares. I felt the style called for straight line quilting, but I softened it with the ivy in the first border. After all the work, I loved the pattern even more."

Fabric Requirements:

3 1/4 yds white (background and border)
1/8 yd very lt blue (A)
1/8 yd lt blue (B)
1 1/2 med blue (C)
1/8 yd of each of the following:
  dk blue (D)
  lt pink (E)
  med pink (F)
  dk pink (G)
  very dk pink (H)
  lt moss green (I)
  bright green (J)
  dk green (K)
  rust brown (L)
  med brown (M)
  dk brown (N)
  bright yellow (O)
  lilac (P)
  purple (S)

Pattern Pieces (pages 59 and 60):

A 1 1/8" square
B Border Triangle
C Border Section
D Center Border Section
E End Border Section (allows for mitering corners)

Cutting Requirements:

1. Cut the following 1 1/8" squares:
  1494 white
  6 very lt blue (A)
  64 lt blue (B)
  119 med blue (C)
  61 dk blue (D)
  22 lt pink (E)
  47 med pink (F)
  23 dk pink (G)
  32 very dk pink (H)
  48 lt moss green (I)
  87 bright green (J)
  36 dk green (K)
  59 rust brown (L)
  103 med brown (M)
  45 dk brown (N)
  24 bright yellow (O)
  30 lilac (P)
  22 purple (S)
2. Cut the following border pieces:
  18 Triangles (B), med blue
  eight Border Sections (C), white
  two Center Border Sections (D), white
  eight End Border Sections (E), white (four are reversed)
3. Cut the following border strips:
  two 2 1/2" 33 1/4", white
  two 2 1/2" x 40 1/4", white
  two 2 1/2" x 41 14", med blue
  two 2 1/2" x 48 1/4", med blue

Instructions

Piecing the Quilt

1. Place squares in rows following placement in **Fig 1** on next page.

2. Sew squares together in rows. Sew pairs of squares; then pairs of pairs and so on until a complete row is sewn.

3. Write row # on a piece of paper and pin to each row after it is sewn.

4. Sew rows together in pairs; then sew pairs together and so on until all rows are sewn together.

Rows

Fig 1

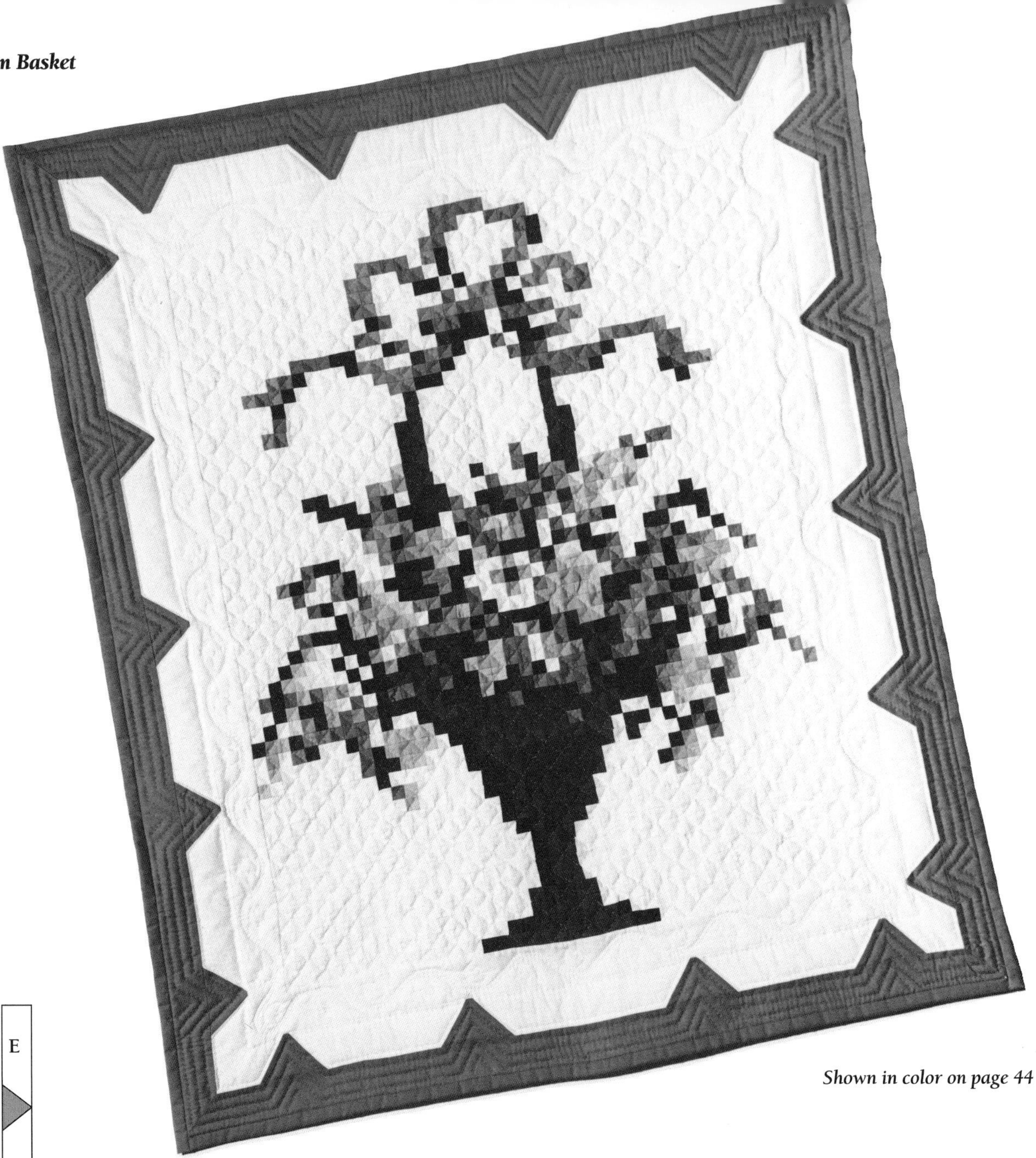

Shown in color on page 44

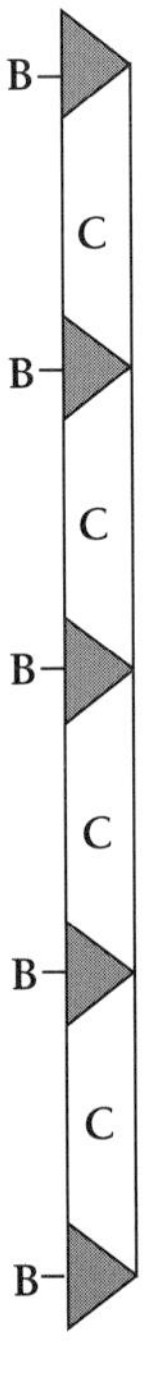
B
C
B
C
B
C
B
C
B

Fig 2

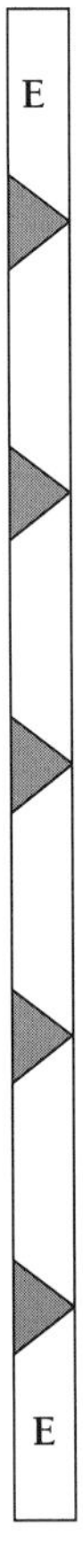
E
E

Fig 3

Adding Borders

1. Add first white border, mitering corners (see steps 2 and 3 of Finishing in *Des Paniers Bleus*, page 54 for mitered corners).

2. For sides of second border, sew five med blue Triangles (B) and four white Side Border Sections (C) together, **Fig 2**. Sew End Section (E) to each end, **Fig 3**.

3. For top and bottom of second border, sew a blue Triangle (B) to each side of white Border Section (C), **Fig 4**; repeat. Sew to each side of Center Border Section (D), **Fig 5**. Sew an End Border Section (E) to each end, **Fig 6**. Sew second border to quilt, mitering corners.

Fig 4

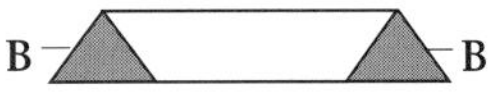
B
B

Fig 5

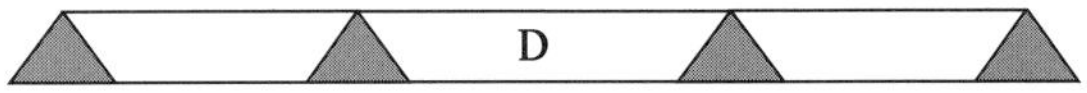
D

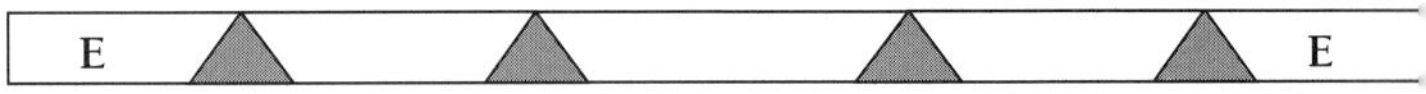
E
E

Fig 6

4. Sew third med blue border to quilt as in steps 1 and 2.

Finishing the Quilt

See General Directions starting with Preparing the Quilt Top, page 6, to finish quilt. Photographed quilt was quilted diagonally through each square of center section. A curvy vine-leaf motif was quilted in the first white border and the final blue border was quilted in straight lines, 1/2" apart and following shape of triangle.

Quilt Layout

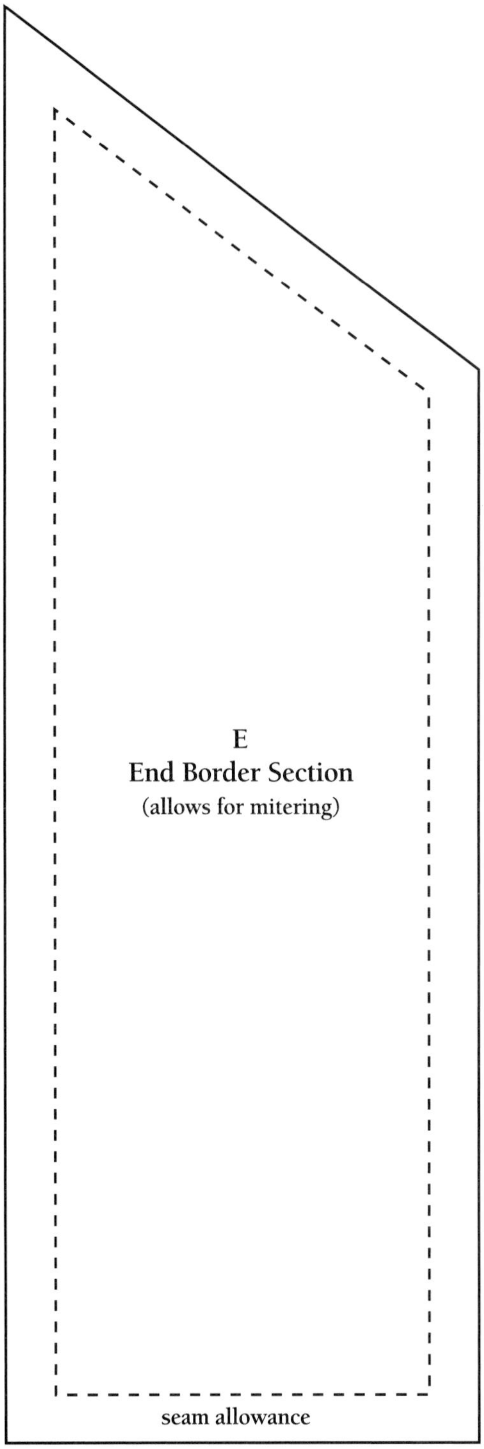
E
End Border Section
(allows for mitering)
seam allowance

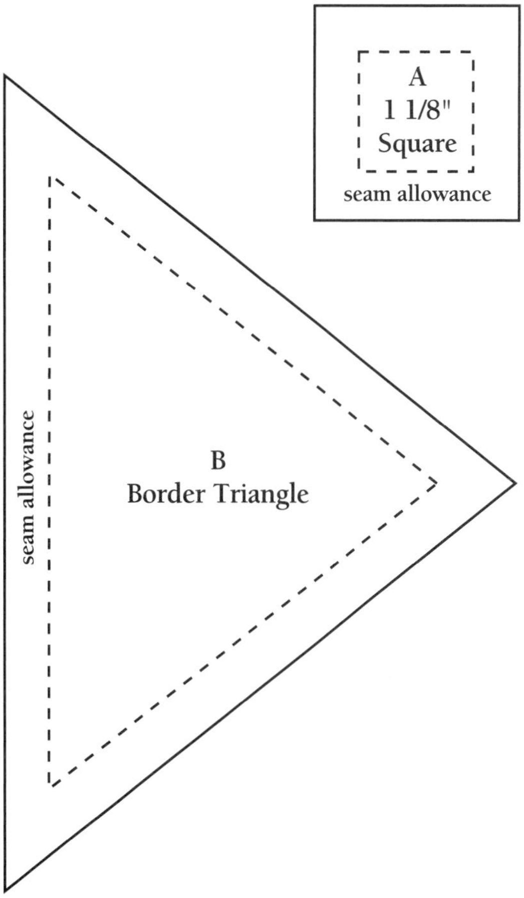
A
1 1/8"
Square
seam allowance
seam allowance
B
Border Triangle

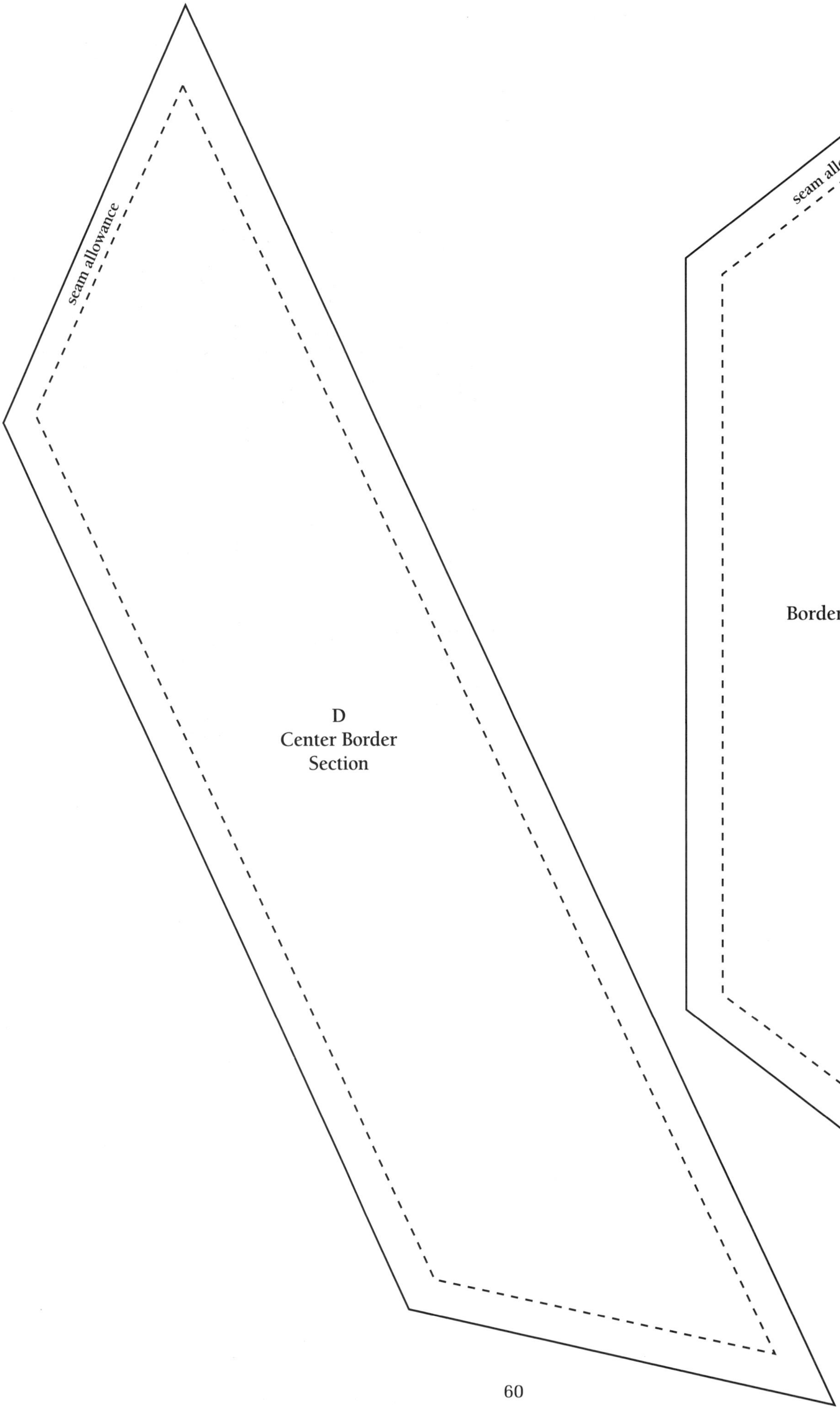
seam allowance
D
Center Border
Section

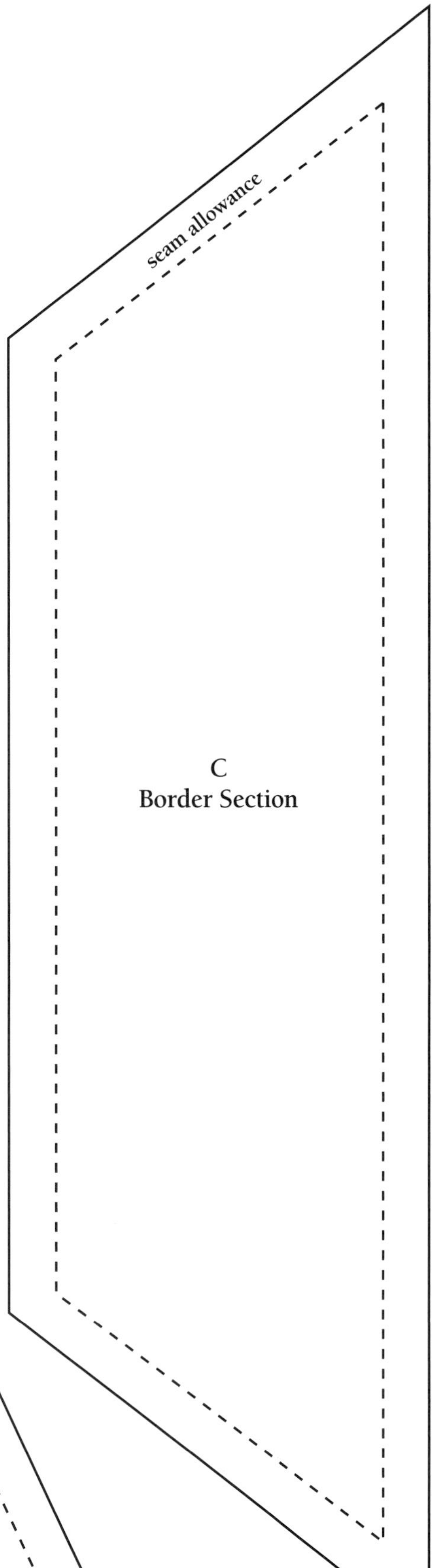
seam allowance
C
Border Section